Advance Praise for Gail F. Meintzer's
Detours

"I liked this book. As a retired member of the US Army who served in some very non-traditional and unique areas, it is a pleasure to read of others who served in unique ways. While my years in uniform were well after Mr. Meintzer's, even then we had soldiers who had special and unique occupations and duties. Reading of his experiences was a joy and he tells the story well. I am also a huge fan of nostalgic normal people history. Anecdotes about growing up in days past are powerful to me. Reading his experiences and stories in some ways was like reading my father's stories. I very much enjoyed reading DETOURS and would recommend it to anyone with an interest in nostalgic American History."

—Don Herrmann, MSG, US Army Retired

"What a delightful read! DETOURS covers the life of an accomplished, successful railroad veteran from a young lad growing up in the Depression-era, who has an inquisitive, searching mind and a loving family, to having a successful career in the railroad industry. It was noteworthy how Mr. Meintzer took lessons from early life and applied them in his varied career. Some of the hijinks he got himself into, both as a kid and as adult in life, were so genuine and entertaining. With a number of health issues being confronted in life, I was left with the impression that Mr. Meintzer indeed has 9 lives! He performed an important service to his family by taking the time to chronicle his life."

—Gordon Jonasson,
Former Superintendent of Transportation, Milwaukee Road

DETOURS

A Memoir of a Railroad Man

Gail F. Meintzer

Category: Men's Memoir/Non-Fiction: Railroad, World War II, and Korean War
Description: *Gail F. Meintzer, a US Army Veteran, shares his philosophies from lessons learned the hard way, as he took the long road less traveled on the iron highway.*
Ebook ISBN: 9780998167374
Paperback ISBN: 9780998167367
Large Print Hardcover ISBN: 9780998167350

First printing by Written Dreams Publishing, November 2016.

Green Bay, WI

*For my wife, Neva, and our children,
for all the times I spent away from you.*

"The Old Milwaukee Road"
—Chris Watkins and Ric Swanson

Dear Reader,

I hope you enjoy the story of my life, both single and married. I would like to say it was interesting. If you'd like to learn more about working on the railroad, go to the National Railroad Museum in Green Bay, Wisconsin. Their library is outstanding and filled with many resources.

Several people asked me why I wrote this book, and I'll try to explain the different reasons now. Since the beginning of writing this book, one thing after another came up in my mind, which I thought should be included in *Detours*.

One of them is the subject of all the aunts and uncles we had growing up that were not related to us. Now I know that most readers will ask *what is he saying?*

Back in my day growing up, you respected your elders and referred to them as Mr. or Mrs., but mostly we referred to them as aunt this or uncle that. We knew all of our neighbors by their first and last names, and it was common courtesy to call them by, for example, Aunt Minnie or Uncle Rudy. Even though we were just young children, our neighbors would stop and talk with us, and they really seemed to care about us. In all of the various places Neva and I have lived during our life span, I've never seen this happen anywhere else. It seems people's values are changing. It's too bad, but it doesn't mean that you, dear reader, have to do so. Take the higher ground. Be respectful, honorable, and honest. That, I promise you, will help you live a life worth living.

Our children know the genealogy of the Meintzer family back into the 1700s, with thanks due to my niece, Christian Bauman, a genealogist. They didn't know how we grew up, as well as my life after high school, WW II, the Korean War, or what went on as they grew up and that is the primary reason why I wrote my story.

Also, my sister, Ardyth, and I talk on a daily basis, as we are concerned about each other due to our advanced ages and various illnesses. During these conversations, different issues came up and questions flew back and forth between us which brings forth, "Why didn't Mother or Dad mention this to us or leave information about things that happened back in their days?" That made me realize that if I didn't do this now, it would be forever lost when I die.

So, under the guidance of my editor and over a period of three to four months, I scoured our albums for pictures, newspaper articles I saved—many more of them previous lost—talked with my sister, my niece, Chris, and started writing in long hand. I tried recording my words, only to find out that turned into a disaster. Finally, I woke up to the fact it would be easier to do it on the computer as I could switch things around and delete my mistakes.

As we have thirteen grandchildren and nine great grandchildren, they, if they are interested, will have this information about what their grandparents did in their days on this earth, as well as some of the health problems that may or may not happen to them through our DNA which passed on.

I hope they will take the time to read this book, and in turn as they grow older, write their memories so their children, grandchildren and great grandchildren will know what happened in their life.

Keep it in the fairway,
Gail F. Meintzer

Christopher and Minnie Meintzer, Sept. 27, 1913

Christian and Sophia Meintzer, pre-1920

Minnie and Chris Meintzer, late 1920s

Ardyth and Gail in the front yard on
Shermer Avenue

Gail and Ardyth Meintzer in Northbrook, IL,
1930s

Gail Meintzer, 3 years old and Ardyth Meintzer,
7 years old

Road conditions in Northbrook, IL, 1930s

Grandma Elfrieda Moeller, early 1940s

Chapter 1

With a raging blizzard snowing in Northbrook, Illinois, a small suburb with a population of 1200 residents approximately 20 miles north of Chicago, it was so bad outside they couldn't get my mother to the hospital. That's exactly when I decided it was time to make my appearance in this world on March 31, 1926, and what an effect it had.

The doctor evidently not thinking he would be called out on such a day had had a snoot full of alcohol, and put the wrong medicine in my eyes after delivering me. Thank God someone noticed and flushed out my eyes, or I would have been blind for the rest of my life.

At that time Mother, Dad and my sister, Ardyth, lived on the second floor of Grandma and Grandpa Moeller's wood-framed house on Church Street in

Northbrook. So when I came along, it got a little crowded.

After I was born, Mother named me Glenn. Where she got that name from, I have no idea, but I would have ended up with the same initials—GFM—whether she had my name changed or not.

Shortly after I was born, a problem cropped up. I couldn't keep anything down in my stomach. It made no difference what it was—mother's milk, cow's milk, formula—nothing would stay down. They should have tried a martini perhaps, a drink I love. Every time I have one, believe me it stays down, just like a scotch and water. (Good thing I had a lot of them when I was young, as I've been advised by my doctors I shouldn't drink them anymore. I have to settle for a glass of red wine now, and only one per day.)

Finally in desperation, as they had to get some nourishment in me, the doctor suggested to my mother to try Borden's Eagle Brand condensed milk. Why not? She'd tried everything else. She bought a few cans of it and tried it out on me. Thank God it worked. Everything stayed down where it belonged and they didn't have to worry any further.

As Mother was looking at the Borden's can, she noticed there was a picture of the president of Borden's on it. The can showed his name as Gail Borden. I understand that he appeared to be about sixty years old, so between the two of us, we've had the name now for 150 years. It's too bad I never had the chance of meeting him. The man saved my life by creating the brand of condensed milk.

Mother was so happy she sent 75 cents into the State of Illinois requesting the name on my birth certificate be change to Gail Frank Meintzer, and I've had it ever since, for the past ninety years.

Our name seems to be very popular as a woman's name, but I wonder if there are any two women who can make their claim to fame as Gail Borden and I can. Now, if there are any women with the name of Gail that reads this, please don't get upset with me as you will see later in the book, I hated the name until my sixteenth year. Even then, I don't have any idea why I decided to take a liking to it. To this day, I still receive mail addressed to Miss or Ms. In fact, when I graduated from high school, I received six different invitations to attend girl schools and my mother would not allow me to go to any of them. Darn! I tried to reason with her that I would major in "studying girls," but she wouldn't have any part of it. After all, it was due to my mother that I ended up with the name Gail; I would have been just as happy with the name Glenn.

Shortly after I was born we moved to Mother and Dad's new one and a half story house that had a stucco exterior on Shermer Avenue in Northbrook. It was only a half block from the restaurant where Mother worked as a Cook and about a block from the school I would attend until I graduated from eighth grade when I was a little older. (It was a good school, but it was small in comparison to some of today's schools my grandchildren and great grandchildren attend.)

***

I had one set of living grandparents when I was born. My dad's mother and father, Sophia and Christian, had lived on a farm in the Riverwood's area west of Deerfield, Illinois. They were both dead before I was born. Grandpa Christian was born April 3rd, 1830 in Dehlingen, Bas-Rhin, Alsace, and Grandma Sophia was born quite a few years later on September 16, 1842 in Lorentzen, Bas-Rhin, Alsace. When they were living in France, he was a Hussar in the French Army.

This history gets a little confusing when it's being discussed at family get-togethers as I believe it's due to the fact that years ago Germany, France and Belgium were at war several times. It depended on who won as to what country you lived in. My understanding is that we were Germans originally. The Meintzer family lived in Bas-Rhin, Alsace, which at that time that Christian Meintzer was alive was occupied by France, otherwise he wouldn't have been in the French Army. That was his only reason to come to America, so his sons would not have to join the military. Several years after they took the boat to the United States, Grandma Meintzer died on September 7, 1913. Grandpa Meintzer lived only a few years without her and passed on January 28, 1922. I don't know much about them, but from the stories my father told they were both hard-working people.

My mother's parents were Karl and Elfriede Moeller. Grandpa Moeller was a crossing guard for the Milwaukee Railroad in Shermerville, which is now Northbrook. At the time Grandpa Moeller was there, the thought of my working for the Milwaukee Road and becoming an official of the company never occurred to me or my parents.

My last recollection of Grandpa Moeller was around the time I was five years old when I saw him lying in bed with the drapes closed. I found out much later in life that he had died of cancer. Grandma Moeller lived for a long time afterward. (She was still alive when Neva and I were married on June 21, 1947.)

My sister, Ardyth, and I used to stop at Grandma's on our way to church. Actually, we were more interested in going to Grandma's than we were to church because of the fresh baked coffee cake that she made for us. She also gave me coffee, but that was a forbidden subject to talk about in those days. I was too young to drink coffee and was told it would stunt my growth. Grandma Moeller was a good baker and her coffee cakes were delicious.

***

One day Ardyth and I went to our church. I remember sitting down to an excellent tasty chicken dinner they held every year, that for some reason I didn't know what it was for, and at my age it didn't matter to me. The chicken dinner was the important thing.

I was having a problem trying to cut the chicken off of the bones when the minister leaned over and said, "Buddy, God made fingers before knives and forks, so you can use them instead to eat that chicken."

And, I did. That was a good idea. I liked that minister; there should be more men like him.

***

My sister and I had light hair and fair complexions, which I think was due to the fact our predecessors were of German heredity. Mother was a good-sized woman with light brown hair and Dad, having worked on his parentss farm and at the brickyard, was thin and wiry. Dad had a bit of an odd sense of humor but no one messed with Mother, no matter the subject. Even Dad.

Our house on Shermer Avenue had two bedrooms. It was okay when Ardyth and I were small enough to sleep in the same bedroom, but when I was five, I moved to the dining room. It had French doors between it and the living room, and I slept on a day bed.

We had a nice, big dog whose name was Cubby, while we lived in that house. She was a black Schnauzer with wiry hair that was really long where her facial hair grew. She was a good watch dog and very protective of our family members.

The dog was in the living room one morning when Dad came in to wake me up. He raised his hand to swat me on the butt gently, but before his hand got to my butt, Cubby had Dad's wrist in his mouth. She didn't bite my father, but she wasn't going to let Dad swat me, either.

With Mother working at the restaurant, and with the Great Depression at its peak, Cubby ate better than any of us. Mother would bring home bones from the restaurant that still had meat on them for Cubby. Cubby enjoyed the bones and we never had to buy dog food. Ever.

Neva and Gail Meintzer, and Bob Haws at
Bartleme's Inn

Chapter 2

When we were a little older and could understand, Mother would tell us of things she experienced when she was the cook at Bartleme's Inn in Northbrook. The stories were fun to listen to and unusual, and I never doubted they were true. The Bartleme's Inn building was large and in the shape of a back word "L". One portion was adjacent to Shermer Avenue—the dining room and bar, and the part adjacent to Waukegan Road, the bar, the family room and the kitchen was adjacent to the family room. Their bedrooms were upstairs. Parking was behind the building, and there was a grove where they could have picnics and pig roasts.

When Mother was cooking, they had an old German man as a waiter. One night after serving a meal, he ran back into the kitchen scared as hell, asking Mother to help him. Before Mother could find out what was happening, Al Capone walked in, and Mother asked what was going on.

Capone said, "I'm trying to tip our waiter for the good job he did, but he won't take the money," which was a $100.00 bill. In those days, that was a lot of money.

Everyone knew who Capone was—the biggest gangster in Chicago—and most were afraid of him. That was why the waiter wouldn't accept such a large tip, thinking Capone would probably shoot him afterwards.

Mother looked at the two of them and told Capone to give her the money. He did, and she turned to the waiter, handing him the money. Then she looked at Capone and told him, "Now get the hell out of my kitchen." And he did. Mother wasn't afraid of anyone.

Another time Mother did something similar. I saw it happen this time in the kitchen of the Briargate Country Club. When I saw what she did, I knew Mother was telling us the truth about the Capone incident. She wouldn't let anyone push her around.

***

The state of Illinois had a law about when school children started school. When I was four years old it was that if you had your fifth birthday during the school year, you could start school when you were four years old. This worked out fine for my mother since she was working. She didn't need a baby sitter because of the hours she worked, but I went to school anyway. It wasn't that great for me, though, as I was the smallest kid in every class I had. Having a birthday on March 31st, the school year was almost over before I turned five years old.

When I was in first grade, the school had a program where all of the classes participated in a sports endeavor. The higher the class, the harder the program for them. Being in first grade, our activity was running a wheelbarrow race.

I was the wheelbarrow going down the floor on the first leg and my partner would be the wheelbarrow on the return trip. When he got down on his hands, he kicked his legs out for me to catch them. I missed his right leg but it didn't miss me, catching me in the wrong spot—my groin. I went down on the floor in agony. We managed to finish the race, but I was still hurting.

When my sister and I got home that afternoon Mother asked me why I had fallen to the floor. After I told her what happened, she examined me right away and said she would have to take me to the doctor the next day, which meant a trip to Chicago on the train.

As the doctor examined me, he advised Mother I should have an operation. Apparently, my testicle had lodged itself up inside me. My partner had definitely had an impact on my groin area with his kick, but it was the Great Depression. There wasn't any money for this type of operation. While it was bad, it wasn't life threatening. The doctor said I probably wouldn't be able to sire any children.

I explained this to Neva, my wife, after we were engaged and she accepted me as I was. However, after I got married I proved the doctor wrong on that score.

This injury had a lasting effect on my life until my retirement, when I had a hernia and asked Doctor Richard McNutt in Green Bay to take care of both problems at the same time. The good doctor did a great job getting everything straightened out and back into place, and removing my testicle. From the time the injury happened until the surgery was a period of seventy-seven years.

Back in the 1930s, doctors didn't have the knowledge they have today, which is too bad, but it wouldn't have helped me anyway since my parents didn't have the money for an operation.

Looking back into time, I can still see my dad in his overalls, with his thin hair, sitting at the kitchen table, reading the newspaper. Mother always wore an apron over her dress, and she'd be sitting across from him doing a crossword puzzle.

When we were young, Ardyth, would sit at the table doing her homework, and I'd be reading a book, with a kerosene lamp furnishing light for all of us. We had electricity, but my folks did their best to keep costs down to a minimum, as times were hard for most families during the Great Depression. Hopefully, this country will never go through another decade like that one.

My sister and I have talked about it periodically. At Christmas and our birthdays, we would get one gift and we were happy with it. We had a garden at the back end of the yard where we grew strawberries, along with assorted vegetables for our dinner table.

Ardyth and I would pick and sell the strawberries for 25 cents a quart to the neighbors in the area. When I think back to that time, I wonder if the neighbors bought the strawberries for eating or to help a needy neighbor, or both. We got by and were all happy, regardless of the circumstances.

***

One of my parents' rules I had to follow was to be home for supper. Any time I would turn the corner into the back yard and saw Dad sitting near the bottom of the stairs, I knew I was late. Dad's foot was going to help me get to the top of the stairs. Thinking back on his actions, I wonder if he would have made a great field goal kicker for a football team. He sure knew how to kick with the side of his shoe.

Mother's suppers tasted good and were filling.

Despite not having a lot of money, my parents always made do with the little they had to keep us kids fed.

One day in school I was causing some trouble by making noises and misbehaving. My teacher wasn't happy by my disturbance and banged the back of my head against the blackboard a few times. It didn't hurt that bad, but it was embarrassing. I didn't say a word about it when I got home from school as I knew what Mother or Dad would do about my being naughty at school.

We knew when we were told to do something there wasn't any quibbling. We did it. Or we were punished. I believe we were like most kids, and occasionally, we did things that weren't the proper things to do. (Back then, they didn't spare the rod, and I still think it was the best way to raise kids.)

One day, my mother asked me to pick up the mail at the post office when I was about six years old. I was standing in line behind the chief of police and noticed the strap over his pistol wasn't locked. I reached over, pulled the gun out, and scared the devil out of everyone, including the chief.

He took it out of my hand and thank God, he didn't tell Mother or Dad. I just wanted to hold it, as I never saw one before and told him so. The chief scolded me gently and sent me on my way. Can you imagine what would have happened if a kid did that in this day and age?

***

We used to ride our bikes all over, as there weren't as many cars and trucks as there are today, but I still had orders from my parents to be careful and stay off the highways.

Well, one day my buddy and I decided to ride to Glenview, Illinois, a town that was about 8 to 10 miles away by highway. When we got there, it was my dumb idea to stop in and say hello to friends of Mother and Dad. You really have to be stupid to do something like that, because by the time I rode home Mother had already heard about it. I got a swift hand to my butt in response. It seemed the older we got, people delighted in keeping our parents advised of what we were doing. Maybe it was because of the things I got myself into, or did.

***

In late spring, a couple of us saw a small barge on the creek that ran through town. It was the kind of barge they used to move cement or gravel up or down a waterway, and as it was empty just floating in the creek, we decided to take a ride down stream. Since it didn't have a motor on it, we used a broken limb to push it off the shore. It was fun for a while, and then we used the limb to get it to the shore. We jumped out and walked home.

It was an act not done maliciously; we thought it would be fun to take a ride and didn't know any better. We were smart enough, for a change, not to tell anyone about it. We also never thought what could have happened to us doing such a silly thing.

About this time in my life I started losing the enamel on my teeth. Why, I have no idea. My teeth actually looked black and Mother took me to the local dentist. Over a period of a few months, he covered my teeth with a white substance. I don't know if it was enamel or something else, but it made them look white and good again. (I always had a lot of trouble with my teeth until I had all of them removed. I have had dentures ever since. Never have a toothache anymore.)

***

In winter time, we did a lot of ice skating. Maintenance crews in town covered the tennis courts with water and it was a great place for the ice rink, as there was also a separate warming room for both the girls and boys.

While you were in the boys room warming up, you could get your sex education listening to the older boys talking about their sexual adventures. I wonder how much truth or wishfulness was actually involved in those stories.

The boys would play ice hockey when it wasn't

crowded, until one day, when I accidently hit a kid in the face with my hockey stick and split his cheek open. He was behind me, so I didn't see him as I was going to hit the puck. The park authorities decided then it was time to end this kind of activity.

The kids' family lived behind our home on the next street, on property Dad sold his family to build their home. After a lot of bleeding and a few stitches, the kid's face was fine.

***

I have a lot of praise for my sister, Ardyth, from the time I was four or five years old until now when we're both in our nineties. She's been a good sister to me. When we were small, Mother would tell her to watch me. So, when Ardyth told me to do something, I did it.

I can recall some incidents when she wanted to go to a school affair. She would ask Dad for the money, usually 10 cents or so, and he would give it to her.

Then I would ask, because I wanted to go, too. Dad would say no, so Ardyth would give back the money to him and say she didn't want to go if Buddy couldn't. Dad would then give me 10 cents, too so I could go to the event. That was the type of sister any brother should want, and I've never forgotten it.

Ardyth and I were talking on the phone recently. When I mentioned this to her, she couldn't remember it. However, it was something I never forgot and never will. I was lucky to have such a wonderful sister who was so thoughtful.

We still call each other to make sure neither of us is having a problem in our daily lives. If either of us did, the other couldn't do anything about it, but it makes us feel better to know about it. Plus, we enjoy talking to each other.

One day when I called to speak to her, Ardyth mentioned that she was thinking about our relationship and couldn't recall a single time we had a fight or argued with each other. When I started to think about it, I couldn't remember a time, either.

While Ardyth and I were talking, the subject of politics came up. She and I found out we did not agree and decided it would be better to not discuss this subject deeply ever again, unless it was on the lighter side. By rule-of-thumb, it turned out to be the right choice for us as siblings.

It's funny how coming from a family of only two children, both of us expanded our families after our weddings to five children each.

There were times when Neva and I would drop off our children at Ardyth and Bob's place or they would drop off their kids at our place. Neva and I would go somewhere to get some rest, as well as peace and quiet. The kids weren't bad, and they all seemed to have fun playing with each other. While they don't see each other often, they're still good friends and are happy to see each other when they get the chance.

***

It was during the last couple of years of living at home when we were ages nine thru twelve that we would caddy at the local golf courses.

Mother asked our local milk man if he would pick me up on his way to work and drop me off at the golf course. The man agreed. He'd pick me up at five in the morning, drop me off at the golf course, so I was usually the first or second one there, and then I'd wait for the golfers to arrive. It was on a first come-first out to caddy basis.

In the afternoons, I'd walked home from the golf course. I could stop at the drug store and buy a chocolate malted milk as Mother wanted me to do, since she said I was so small and skinny. Then when I arrived home, I gave the rest of the money to Mother to keep. I made a dollar for caddying eighteen holes and was glad when I got a quarter for a tip. It was nothing compared to the prices and tips caddies receive today, but it was good money then.

I'll never forget the time I was hitch-hiking home

from Northbrook Golf Course and three fellows in a convertible picked me up. They asked where I was going.

I told them where I had to get off, and the driver said, "Hell, we're going to take you further than that," and the rest of them agreed. They kept talking about what they were going to do to me as far as taking me further the entire ride.

Talk about being scared, believe me I was.

The driver did stop the car where I had to get off, laughing about it, but it took me a long time to get over it. They might have thought it was funny to scare people, but I sure didn't. I thought twice before getting into somebody's car after that happened.

***

Somehow, I was given the nickname of "Buddy" or "Bud" and no one called me Gail until I was a teenager. I didn't mind it, but my first problem happened when I was graduating from grade school in 1939.

The teacher asked my class what name we wanted on our certificates. I told her "Bud Meintzer".

I can't figure out why they would ask us kids what name should be on the certificates rather than our parents for this kind of information. We were told it had to be our given name, and not wanting

Gail on it, I told them to use Frank Meintzer, as Frank was my middle name.

My mother was not a happy camper when they announced Frank Meintzer during the ceremony. She asked those around her who Frank Meintzer was as I proudly walked up to get my certificate.

Did I ever catch hell when it was over and I had to join my family to go home. It wasn't a happy trip home for me at all.

***

It was about this time that Mother and Father signed a contract to run the dining room and bar at Briargate Country Club in Deerfield, Illinois. They sold their house in Northbrook, and we moved into the cottage next to the clubhouse on the golf course. Cubby came, too. There were two bedrooms on the second floor; Ardyth had one and I had the other one. The bathroom was also up there.

Downstairs, Mother and Dad used the dining room as their bedroom. We had a living room and a kitchen. We also had a basement under the house.

When our dog had distemper and started foaming at the mouth, we put her down in the basement. Then we called the police to have her put down. I don't remember knowing about a veterinarian in town.

My sister stayed at a girlfriend's home in

Northbrook during the week and came home on the weekends, while I rode my bike back and forth to Northbrook until the school year was finished. I graduated from 8th grade that May and Ardyth was a junior.

Then we both went to high school in Highland Park the following school year. Ardyth was in the senior class and I was a freshman.

At the time we moved to the cottage, a bowling alley was built and I got a job setting pins with a chance to learn how to bowl.

I didn't think too much about setting pins, until one day in school when my mind was wandering— it did that a lot—I started to think about it. An average bowling pin weighed 3 pounds and a bowling ball usually weighed 16 pounds. When I figured five people to a team, two teams on my two alleys for three games, plus an average game score a bowler had was 150. That would total over several thousand pounds in one night of setting pins. No wonder we were tired.

There were a few other boys who set pins with me. What really helped us to become good bowlers was the owner allowed us to bowl free every Saturday morning, as long as we would set pins for each other and he didn't need to pay us for it. The free bowling was our pay. He watched us and noticed who was turning out to be the best bowlers, and I was one of the better ones.

I believe being small and not built to play football or basketball, I put more effort into bowling and golf as I could compete with anyone, which I did.

When I was sixteen, I met a young man from the North Shore area, who bowled at our bowling alley. He liked bowling for money, and it's nice to say he kept me in the money for a long time before he realized it was a losing proposition before he decided not to come back again.

George Moen, another guy I met setting pins, (who a few years later in my life was the best man at my wedding,) was also a good bowler. We teamed up and were ready to take on any one who was interested in bowling for money. Fortunately, we made quite a bit of money doing it.

Later on, when I started working for the railroad, I was making more money bowling than I was working for the railroad. Of course, that changed as I was promoted into higher paying positions within the railroad company.

We also played for money on an individual basis while we were in high school. Bowling as a team, the winner was based on a three-game total of the team. Individually, it was based on a five-game total per man. While some people may frown on it, we always made sure we never beat any opponents by too large a total so we didn't drive them away. Anytime it was a close game, they wanted to try again and we were happy to oblige them.

Once in a while we'd lose and it cost us money. However, most of the time it worked in our favor.

***

When I entered Highland Park High School in 1939, I did it under the name of G. Frank Meintzer. In the Alumni Directory of 2014, I noticed they had me listed as Gail F. Meintzer, class of 1943.

In high school, I didn't participate in any school sports as I didn't have the large size to do it. I got off to a bad start my freshman year when I was sick for four weeks and was told I would either have to make up the work or take the tests to see what happens. I decided to take the tests and hope for the best.

It didn't go well.

Flunking Algebra, English and Spanish the first term as a freshman was not the best thing to do. Thank the Lord, I finished the rest of the year with grades good enough to offset the first term and passed all of my courses.

During my sophomore year I took Geometry, which I barely passed, General Science, English, and History, which I enjoyed. I also had Mechanical Drawing, Typing and some shop classes that finished out my day.

In my junior year, I signed up for Science, English, History, Auto Mechanics, and more shop classes.

During one of my shop classes, I built a bob-sled that would hold about five riders. We didn't have any decent hills to go down, but the idea was to attach a long rope from the sled and be pulled by a car by looping the rope around the car bumper so we could let loose of the rope if we wanted to. We had a highway going through the village, but not much traffic, so normally we didn't anticipate any trouble. Although, we did have our close calls once in a while.

I can still recall one night when my friends and I were on Waukegan Road, the highway that goes through town. We were going north and decided to go to the other side of the road. We saw a semi-truck coming southbound toward us.

One of my friends hollered to let loose of the rope, but I yelled no as we would lose our momentum and would be run over by the truck. We narrowly missed the truck by a few feet, but the scare slowed us down on our winter activities for a while.

In my senior year, I only had one class that was mandatory—American History. All of the other classes I took that year were shop classes. Still, I loved American History and it was the last class of the day. Going into the final class with A's in all of my shop classes, by the end of the first grading period, I'd made the honor roll for the first time.

All of my papers and tests were graded as A's in History.

And then the roof fell in.

My teacher put a B on my report card. Naturally, I questioned the grade and asked why. She was a nice, young teacher who always sat on the front edge of her desk during classes wearing a skirt, and us young lads of seventeen and eighteen enjoyed the scenery. She told me that since I never spoke in class, she had lowered the grade for not participating. I couldn't tell her why I didn't participate because I was spending my time looking. Instead I said, "Well, you might as well write B across the card for the year and I can forget this class."

She sent me to the Dean's office for a little chat with him for that remark. I did get B's in all of the grading periods for the rest of the year in her class.

One thing I realized as I experienced high school was the fact the teachers were trying to prepare my class for college. I thought was a lost cause, as most of us were going to be drafted into World War II and didn't know whether we would come back alive or not.

Because I had started school at the age of four, when I graduated from high school I was the second youngest graduate in a class of 257 graduates. I was seventeen years, one month and a half old.

After I graduated, I have never used Algebra or Geometry again. It would have been better for me to take Business Math, as that is a subject everyone has to use during their entire lifetime.

***

It was a lot of fun for the three years we lived on the golf course. I helped Dad in the Bar Room, bringing in cases of bottled beer and soda, as well as waiting on tables and serving drinks. This was before there were laws prohibiting minors from doing these things. In addition I caddied, and when we had large golf outings, I would help in the kitchen, putting dishes and silverware thru the dishwasher after they were scraped off.

After everything was cleaned up, Mother would furnish dinner to all of the helpers. They asked for steaks but I wanted ham. I could never figure out why the other waiters were always laughing and smiling at me when I said I wanted ham. Of course it's a matter of opinion, but I learned later on in life that steak is much better tasting than ham when grilled correctly.

While we were living on the course, I met Bob Haws. He was a local fellow not quite as tall as me with green eyes, brown hair, and a happy disposition as he was always laughing, smiling, or grinning.

One Saturday Bob and I were in line to caddy for a foursome of golfers. It was the Japanese Consul from Chicago, his white wife, and two of his associates from the consulate. We each carried double, and as the golfers were fairly good, we had no problems caddying for them. They liked to play 36 holes each Saturday, stopping to eat lunch between the two rounds.

We received $1.25 per round per bag and a tip, which was usually 25 cents per round per bag. Big money back then and nothing compared to what the caddies get now. The Japanese golfers liked the job we did and we got them as "loops" every Saturday for the rest of the golfing year, as well as the next year which was 1940. But they never showed up the following year. That was the year 1941, when the Japanese bombed Pearl Harbor on December 7.

(By the way, Bob Haws married my sister, Ardyth. He served in the US Navy in World War II and he was one terrific brother-in-law. They didn't come any better.)

***

While we were living at the club, one of the fellows got his mother's car. That night we went to see the movie in Highland Park. After the movie was over, we piled into the car. I sat in the front passenger seat next to the driver, and another fellow was in the back.

The Chicago, Milwaukee and North Shore Electric Line (railroad) ran north and south across the street leading back to Deerfield. There were no signals at the crossing as they usually stopped the train and proceeded as traffic allowed.

We didn't see a train coming until it hit the back end of the car and pushed us sideways over the tracks. It was going so slow none of us got hurt, but as there was damage involved, the police wrote it up. We went home and I forgot to tell Mother and Dad about it.

I suppose I really didn't forget. I just thought it would be better to keep my mouth shut. That isn't the smartest thing to do, either, as sooner or later something happens to bring out the truth and people find out anyway.

About a month later I was out caddying. When I'd finished and went into the kitchen to get something to eat, I saw Mother holding a letter from the railroad. It was addressed to me, but my parents had learned the truth. I was in trouble again.

I wasn't grounded, but Mother wasn't happy with her favorite son. Of course I didn't have any brothers, so I couldn't lose that favorite spot. My only sister, Ardyth, was the favorite daughter. What a team we were.

While we lived at the club, Ardyth had a white cotton jacket she would wear all the time. If celebrities stopped by the club, she would ask them to sign the jacket. She'd then sew over the signature with a different colored thread for each signature.

Ardyth has kept the jacket all these years. I asked her about it the other day and she told me she had given it to her youngest daughter, Christine. I was looking for a particular signature, so I called and asked Chris about it.

She sent me several pictures, showing the names of Johnnie Gottselig, who played hockey with the Chicago Blackhawks. (This was the one I was looking for.) Some of the others were Bob Crosby, (Bing Crosby's brother), Arthur Murray of Arthur Murray Dance Studios, Leo (Gabby) Hartnett who was the catcher for the Chicago Cubs, and Jack Manders, who played for the Chicago Bears. Of course, Ardyth has my signature on it as well. I wasn't missing any chance to get my name on something with the big boys.

Chris still has the jacket and she told me some of the threading is missing. Keep in mind though that it lasted seventy-seven years.

***

We had many functions on the golf course. It was during one of these large golf outings when I saw Mother lose her temper with a customer. There was a group that requested what they wanted for dinner after a round of golf. Their chairman had told Mother they would have 225 people there for steak dinners.

So, Mother then ordered 250 steaks from her purveyor in Chicago, as it gave her a cushion if she needed more. They could still be used in normal business hours if they weren't needed. As the evening wore on, Mother received orders for much more than 225 steak dinners. She used up the extra steaks she ordered, plus a few she had in the coolers. Still, the orders came in.

Although we searched for him, she couldn't find the chairman of the group to tell him there was a problem. Finally, she had to put out ground steak patties.

Naturally complaints got to the chairman and he came in the kitchen to raise hell with my mother.

She told him he had said 225 meals were needed for the event, and she had already sent out over 250 dinners with orders still coming in.

When Mother asked him where these new orders were coming from he admitted he had sold more tickets all afternoon without telling anyone.

Mother ripped into him, saying if he would have had enough brains to say something in the afternoon to her, she could have increased her order. There wouldn't have been any problems, and furthermore, he was paying for every dinner she put out—even if it wasn't a steak at the price agreed upon.

And he did.

As I mentioned earlier, Mother would stand her ground against anyone. I admired that about her.

***

There were several nice things about living on the course, such as the opportunity of playing golf when playtime was light. Plus, the Golf Pro shop sold me clubs that were lost and then found on the course for 50 cents to a dollar. And I bought them until I had a set of unmatched clubs.

One of my responsibilities was going out in the "rough" or out-of-bounds areas to look for lost balls. It cleared the golf course of any lost balls and I got to keep the balls to play with as we didn't have the money to buy golf balls. Even now, I still look for lost balls when I play. Once a Ball Hawk always a Ball Hawk.

Getting the opportunity to play golf when I didn't have work to do was a wonderful thing. I took advantage of it as often as I could, and while I couldn't always play nine or eighteen holes, I would go out to play two, four, or five holes in a short period of time. Normally, this would mean playing the holes that were side by side with each other—1 and 9, 10 and 18, for instance.

Periodically the Pro shop guys would advise me to change things about my game that I wasn't doing properly. I was on the 1st tee one time, taking about seven or eight practice swings when one of the pros asked me if I did that on all my shots.

When I answered, yes, he said, "You should be tired by the time you get done playing."

A lesson well learned. Ever since to this day, I

never take more than one or two practice swings. By the time we moved away from the golf course, I was shooting in the high 70s and low 80s.

After I retired, I still played over a hundred 18-hole rounds of golf each year. As I was aging, I noticed I wasn't hitting the ball as far as I used to, but I still managed to shoot my age at Mid Valley Golf Course when I was 75, and I shot a 78 when I was seventy-nine years old at Irish Waters Golf Course in Freedom, Wisconsin. I've had two holes-in-one and eight eagles in my career.

My first eagle was at Shorewood Golf Course in Green Bay, when it was an 18-hole course. I was playing with a customer, who was also a good friend. The hole was approximately 505 yards long and both of us used our drivers. When we got to our balls, we both used our 4 woods and ended up on the green; he near the front and I at the back of the green about 90 feet from the hole. I was lucky and sunk my putt for an eagle. He missed his first putt and made the second putt for a Birdie. Laughing, he had turned to me and asked, "Don't you ever let a customer win?"

I replied, "You know I could putt one hundred times from there and never make it or even get close. It was just my time to shine."

While I was in my eighties, I managed to continue shooting my age until I was eighty-three. I've played less and less golf as I get older. Last year, I only played 12 rounds of golf on the local courses and those were 9 hole rounds.

Now, in my twilight years, my legs, even using a riding cart, only allow me to play 9 holes at a time. Having to help my wife with her illnesses stops me from playing very often. But it was fun years ago and I don't regret playing less now. Several times in 2015 I had to stop before I finished the round, as I was getting light-headed. I didn't want to take any chance of playing further.

Being a good golfer assisted me when I was working for the railroad while I was in Sales and Marketing. Back then, any time you had a customer on the golf course, he was a captive audience as there weren't any interruptions like phone calls or someone walking into their office. I don't know the reason for it, but looking back over my career I've noticed that most people seem to be enthralled when they can be associated with a person that is good at a sport.

***

There was a local tavern in our town of Deerfield that was not only a sore spot, but also caused problems, making the local people upset. They circulated a petition to stop the sale of liquor in town rather than try to close down that specific tavern.

The owner of the local grocery store signed the

petition, and as petitions are public, Mother went to the Village Hall to see who had signed it. When she saw the signature of the store owner, she made a quick trip to the store for a face-to-face visit with the owner.

Mother bought all of the meat she needed from a purveyor in Chicago, as they had walk-in coolers where she could hang sides of beef. She bought her vegetables from the local grocery store. A weekly bill for vegetables in the summer cost around $300.00.

The owner tried to apologize, but my mother wouldn't have any of it. Mother told him that since he was trying to put her out of business, he wouldn't be getting any more of her business. Mother was true to her word and went elsewhere for her groceries.

That was our last year of living at the golf course, as my folks couldn't make enough money if they couldn't sell liquor there. So, they closed up the restaurant and found a different place to live.

Many years later Mother got another chance to give her opinion to that same grocer.

After Neva and I got married, Neva bought a large beef roast from him and invited Mother and Dad over to our trailer for dinner. Neva had the roast in for more than enough time but it was still so tough she couldn't cut it. Mother took a look at it and asked where she got it.

I said we got it at the grocery store in Deerfield. She told Neva to bring it over to their place on Monday, and they would take us out for dinner Sunday night.

Neva brought it over on Monday and Mother said, "I'm going to take care of this; come with me."

Neva followed her.

Mother took the first step into the store and she hollered to Ed. As he came from the back of the store, she put the roast on the counter and told him, "This is my daughter-in-law and you better never sell her another lousy roast like this."

Neva was so embarrassed she didn't know what to say or do. She couldn't get out of there fast enough. Neva had been with my mother a number of times, but Mother never had a reason to get mad until then. It was a different side of her that Neva saw.

***

I dated girls occasionally in high school and most of the time, I went out with friends in groups. Since the war was on, there was gas and tire rationing and most of us couldn't use a car. Some of my friends spent a lot more time bowling rather than dating, as there wasn't a lot to do in a small village when they couldn't drive a car due to the gas rationing.

When we did go out, we frequently stopped at

Parkside Restaurant to eat. It was a nice restaurant between Deerfield and Highland Park, and quite popular. Most teenagers didn't leave much of a tip, if any, because money was so tight.

Living on the golf course and seeing what happened in the club house by working in the kitchen and dining room, I would tell the fellows to chip in with enough money so we could send a tip to the cook with our order, as I knew the cook would be surprised. They never receive direct tips, and I was sure we would get better service than anyone else.

When the waitress brought our food out with a smile on her face, the looks on the faces of the other customers was priceless. Those customers had been there before us, but we received our food faster than they had. We got a real kick out of it. You get what you pay for, although I don't know if that would occur now.

Gail Meintzer, age 18, June 1944

Gail Meintzer, 1946 in Fort Sill, Oklahoma in S-3 Operations

Gail Meintzer, Tech-5 Rank, Late 1946

Chapter 3

In my third year in high school, World War II was happening so I tried to enlist in the Army Air Corp. I failed the physical when the last doctor who examined me noticed the problem I had had since first grade—the accident during the wheelbarrow race when I was kicked in the groin.

The doctor advised me, and said, "Don't worry. The Army isn't as strict as we are. They will get you when you're eighteen."

And they did.

It didn't bother the medics when they examined me for the draft, but it became an issue much later.

When I graduated from high school, I had just turned seventeen. I decided to take a post graduate course in Mechanical drawing and Blue Print reading, never realizing the effect it would have later in life, helping me when I worked for the railroad.

I attended a school in Rockford, Illinois so I could learn to be a machinist. After a month in school, I had blood poison in my left arm. When the doctor operated on it, I was advised to forget that type of work as they thought I was allergic to the type of oil that is used in machinist work. They couldn't find anything in my blood that would cause me to get blood poison.

It was a Catholic hospital and the nurses were all nuns. After the operation that night the head nurse told me I was to have a sleeping pill to help me sleep.

I said, "I don't want or need a sleeping pill to sleep."

But she insisted, so I took it.

The next morning when I woke up, there were several nurses around my bed, including that head nurse, who was saying words I didn't think nuns would say.

They had my bed cranked so my head was up, my rear was down and my knees were up. They were trying everything to wake me up. It must have scared the hell out of them when they couldn't wake me up.

The head nurse told the other nuns not to give me another sleeping pill under any circumstances, as if it was her fault that I had a sleeping pill the night before.

Eventually I returned home. I heard there was a job opening on the Milwaukee Road in the Chicago Union Station so I went and applied for it. Jobs were opening all of the time, as a lot of fellows were being drafted for the military.

This particular job was as a messenger for the Central Typing Bureau. I worked there for a week before I heard of another job as a mail sorter in the company mail room.

I had the mail room job for two weeks when the office boys' job opened in an auditor's office and I was given that job. This was the job where I met my lovely Neva for the first time, never realizing at that time she would later become my wife.

I hadn't expected to jump from job to job in the railroad, but each time I applied, the pay was better so I took the job. I'm glad I had the opportunity to do that, though. It helped me understand so much more about the workings of the company early in my career than I may have understood otherwise.

***

One day while I was in the office, one of the men stopped me and asked a question that floored me. I didn't realize it, but he also lived in Deerfield— right across the street from where a particular young lady lived. He asked me what was going on between us. I told him and he said as he looked out

58

his front window he would see a young lad leave at about 6 p.m., another lad (me) come about 7 p.m. and leave about 8:45 p.m., and a third young lad about 9 p.m., leaving around 11 p.m.

From what he said, I knew who each lad was. The one from 4 to 6 p.m. went to visit after coming home from school and had to leave so he could start setting pins at the bowling alley by 6:30 p.m.

I went home after work. I ate, cleaned myself up, and then went over to her house before I left to start bowling at 9 p.m.

The third lad was bowling in the 7 p.m. league and was free to visit her after 9 p.m. All three of us were close friends and didn't realize what was happening. As soon as I told them what was going on, the young lady didn't have three young men visiting her every night, or at least they weren't us.

All three of us served in the military, both of my friends went into the Army Air Force, and I served in the Army. The other two young men died a number of years ago, one by suicide and the other by a heart attack just prior to his 50th wedding anniversary. Both were good men.

***

Neva was a messenger in the Wire Room, a place where they would bring in wires for various people. At the time I knew her but I never asked her for a date because she lived in Elgin, Illinois, whereas I lived in Deerfield. We were about 35 miles apart and I didn't have a car to use on account the gasoline rationing was still in effect during the war. My dad had a C-Ration card, since he worked in a Defense plant, which was the best ration card to have for a car, but I would have gotten in trouble if I used his car for my own purposes. While World War II was happening, there was rationing on gasoline, sugar, shoes, meat, tires, etc. as the list goes on, and taxes were from 23% to as high as 94% on some of the wealthiest people. These taxes were meant to pay for the many expenses of World War II.

I wanted to go out with Neva, but I didn't have the means to do it, so why ask her. How would we see each other when we lived so far away?

***

On the train going home from work one day I was reading one of Chicago's newspapers and saw an article about a young man, Jim Neufeldt, who was taking on young bowlers. Jim was undefeated.

After supper, I headed for the bowling alley to show the article to the owner of the alley and asked him what he thought about it.

His reply was picking up the phone, calling the number in the article and setting up a home and home match, starting at our alley and finishing at

Cascade Lanes, which was Jim's home alley, a week later.

It was a packed house there to watch the match. When we finished the games, I was ahead by 35 to 40 pins, which wasn't a lot to take to his alley. The following Saturday night we bowled at Cascade Lanes. It was a close match, with Jim being ahead by several pins, going into the final two frames.

As he finished bowling first, the score sheet indicated I needed a strike in the ninth frame and in the tenth frame two strikes and a good count on the final ball to win. Not the easiest thing to do.

I did get a strike in the ninth frame and one on the first ball in the tenth frame. I still had a chance and needed this next ball to go my way.

When I rolled the ball, it was on track to bury in the pocket for a strike. As it was about to hit the pocket, I started to back-track and ran into John, the owner of our alley, as he was behind me, excited as I was. I had a large count on the next ball and won the match by a few pins. Wow, what a feeling.

Jim was a good sport, even though I had beaten him.

I had noticed three young men watching with a lot of interest, but not pulling for Jim or myself while we were bowling. When we finished the game, Jim asked me to meet them.

I found out the three men were members of the Cascade Kids bowling team from Chicago and were interested in seeing if I was good enough to be on their team. After what they saw when the pressure was on, they asked me to bowl on their team.

I didn't hesitate and really enjoyed the opportunity of bowling with them, until I was drafted into the US Army.

***

The first match I bowled with the team was against the Marigold Kids team at Marigold Arcade in Chicago. We were rolling a few balls for practice before the match started. The captain of our team came over to me and said, "Give me $20.00 for your share. We're bowling for $100.00 per team."

We beat the Marigold Kids so bad that when they came to Cascade Lanes to bowl the following Saturday they wouldn't bet any money. This is a perfect example of how I mentioned earlier in the book about not beating an opponent too badly. But it didn't stop us from bowling well that night.

However, the draft board ruled our captain as 4F meaning unfit for service, and his doctor advised him not to bowl anymore, as he had heart problems. He loved the game so much he ignored the doctor's advice and continued to bowl.

While I was serving in the US Army, I received a letter telling me that after they bowled in a league one night, the fellows bowling in the following league came out to the parking lot to go home. They found our captain slumped over the steering wheel of his car, dead from a heart attack. The love of the game was too much for him.

(I'll never know for sure, but I honestly think if it wasn't for the war I would have had a chance to become a professional bowler. What an amazing effect that would have been on my life only God knows, but I'm happy with the way my life has turned out and how it's ending.)

***

One evening when I was about seventeen, Mother wanted to visit a relative in Des Plaines, Illinois so I drove her over and sat around listening to them talking. Our relative mentioned to me that a girl's family had moved from their village to our village, and warned me not to date her. Supposedly, she was a "fast girl", and they kept talking on and on about her.

Talk about throwing gasoline on a fire. I couldn't wait to get home and try to get this girl out for a date.

I met her and indeed, she was an exciting young lady to go out with on a date. There was no doubt that things could get out of hand very easily. One date was enough for me, as I knew I'd end up in trouble if I continued to date her.

I learned there were two types of girls. The kind you brought home and introduced to your mother and the type you didn't. Believe me, this girl was in the latter group, and I made sure Mother didn't know I had dated her.

Gail Meintzer, US Army, 1945

Gail Meintzer, PFC, 1945 as an MP in California

Chapter 4

The draft board notified me to report for induction, so I reported in to the draft board in Highland Park, Illinois, and met a fellow I went to school with at Highland Park High School. Feeling a little lonely, we agreed to write to the same girl and give her our military addresses so she could pass them on to us so my friend and I could keep in touch.

I never realized the surprise I would receive about six months later. I was assigned to one of the batteries in the 7th Field Artillery Training Regiment at Fort Sill, Oklahoma. The weapons we trained on were the 105mm Howitzers that lobbed a shell 5 to 7 miles, depending on the amount of charge used, as well as the degree that the barrel of the gun was raised. We also carried a 30 caliber carbine.

I received a letter from the girl telling me my friend was killed in action in Germany. The very next day, I received a letter from him telling me what a good time he was having in Germany.

A letter from a dead man makes you feel a little funny, even though I knew he wrote it several weeks before he was killed. The letters gave me pause to reflect as to how lucky I was to be still in the States.

I didn't find basic training difficult. It's true we had to crawl through mud under machine guns firing bullets over our heads, dynamite blowing up alongside of us, and with the NCO's screaming at us to keep our heads down. Having personal hygiene time just before lunch, sometimes it could stop an appetite real fast, like the effect tear gas had, physical training, or firing different types of weapons, etc. Body odor was powerful after training all day.

What scared me was the time we went on a ten-mile hike to a bivouac area and spent a week out in the field. A fellow by the name of Eddie from Indiana was my tent mate. We each had a shelter half to make our tent, and after putting it up, we thought we were all set. That was…until we had mail call.

Each of us had mail so we went head first into the tent, letters in hand, and started reading. Then, we spotted a tarantula crawling under the tent side and we evacuated the tent real fast. I never slept in the tent for the rest of the week. Instead, I slept in the back end of a truck, hoping another tarantula couldn't crawl up the side of the truck. One thing I can't stand are spiders and snakes.

A few days later we were picked for guard duty on the perimeter of the bivouac area. When we reached the area and our post, the first guard took four or five steps and heard the rattle of a rattle snake. The squad leader jumped back into the man behind him. When we saw what was happening, we jumped to the side so we wouldn't get knocked down. We moved away from the area as far as we could so the rattler had plenty of room.

Later that day, I started to get stomach cramps but didn't have time to get to the latrine, so I looked for a good size rock to use. After I rolled the rock out of the hole underneath it, I used the hole to relieve myself. I mean, why not? It was a perfectly good hole.

Evidently an officer in the bivouac area saw what I was doing. Within a few minutes they pulled up in a jeep and asked what I was doing and why I hadn't signaled to be relieved.

I told them I didn't have time, and that I did what the Army Field Manual said to do. I was really glad I had read the manual.

There wasn't anything they could say, so they got back in the jeep and took off.

After the week ended, we went to the barracks at Fort Sill for more training.

A few days after we got back, I was ordered to report to a colonel at the base hospital. He advised me that I should have an operation on my groin to correct what happened to me when I was five years old.

I responded, "The US Army accepted me this way, Sir, and I have done everything the rest of the troops have done and was not left behind at any time, so I see no reason to submit to an operation."

The colonel told me they couldn't force me to have the operation. It had to be my decision, but it would be to my benefit to have it done as it wouldn't cost me any money like it would if I have it done as a civilian after I got out of the army.

I said, "If it gets to the point where I can't do what I'm ordered to do, then I'll submit to the operation."

He ordered me to report back to my unit and there was never any further talk about it.

After a few more weeks of basic training, I was assigned as a clerk typist in the Regimental Headquarters of the 7th Field Artillery Training Regiment.

After a couple of months I wrote up a buck slip to my commanding officer, who was the Adjutant of the Regiment, requesting I be transferred to Paratrooper School so I could be sent overseas to fight.

He called me to his desk, the buck slip in his hand, and told me I was needed just as much here as I would be in the paratroopers. With that said, he tore up the buck slip and dropped it in the waste basket. Then, he told me to get back to work.

Since I didn't get a furlough after basic training, I was given a 10 day furlough so I could be home for Christmas. Just prior to that, I put in an entry to bowl in the Oklahoma City Times Single Classic Bowling Tournament. I was scheduled to bowl on the first Sunday of January, 1945, in the second to last group of bowlers. (Any time I bowled in a tournament, I wanted to bowl as close to the end as possible so I would know what I had to beat to win the tournament.)

I was enjoying my time at home, but knew I had to leave a few days early so I could be in Oklahoma City in time to bowl.

The owner of the Lawton Bowling Alley was also there and he volunteered to give me a ride back to camp when we were finished in the bowling tournament. I knew him quite well, as I spent a lot of nights practicing at his alleys in Lawton.

Finally, it was our time to bowl. I finished the first three games with a 182, 225 and 246 for a 653 series. I needed a series of 615 for the last three games to win the tournament.

While I was rolling the ball good and hitting the 1-3 pocket, I wasn't getting the strikes I needed to score high. I finished with games of 187, 177 and 188 for a total of 552, with a grand total of 1205 for the six games.

After the last squad bowled, we knew I had won

second place in the tournament with a $100.00 prize so we left for Lawton and Fort Sill.

Even though I didn't have to report back to camp until Monday night, I got in late Sunday night and went to bed without a care in the world.

That was…until Monday morning when one of the fellows came back from headquarters, shaking me to wake up.

I mumbled something about still being on furlough and heard in reply, "The colonel wants you now. You better get there."

I dressed in my Class A uniform and reported to our commanding officer, stating that I understood I was supposed to report to the colonel. I explained that I didn't know why, as I was technically still on furlough and hadn't done anything wrong that I knew of.

The man laughed and said, "With your name and our headquarters name all over the newspapers today because of you, yes, the colonel wants to talk to you." And he led me into the colonel's office.

The colonel congratulated me on the recognition I brought to his Regiment, and had another officer set up a Post Photographer to stage a picture of me bowling.

The colonel wanted to push the bowling angle, so we formed a bowling team and put out a notice throughout the post that we would take on any group that was interested.

During that time I had several newspaper articles written about me, regarding my bowling status. Here's a few headlines:

Training Center Soldier Finishes
Second in
Oklahoma Times Tourney

Fort Sill Kegler Is Classic Threat:
Meintzer Has
3-Game 653; Wagle Falters

I was promoted to PFC (Private first class) and transferred to the S-3 section of the Regiment in our headquarters. S-3 covers plans and training of the recruits. The training program included many hours on different subjects, such as firing various weapons—105mm Howitzers, 30 caliber carbines, both 30 and 50 caliber machine guns, hand grenades, personal hygiene, hiking, guard duty, and more, etc.

It was our job to set up the schedules for each platoon in each battery in each battalion in the Regiment. When we made the schedule for firing of weapons or hikes, we had to contact Post S-3 headquarters for approval as other Regiments might be using the same area. We couldn't take the chance of putting the troops in a precarious position, though miscommunications did happen on occasion.

Around noon one day a lieutenant came running in to headquarters, yelling, "They're shooting shells over our heads."

Foul language was spouted as I asked him where the troops were. He said he had told them to lie down, and I told him to "Get 'em out of there!" and bring the troops in to the barracks.

Then I contacted Post Headquarters S-3 Division, telling them "You gave us permission to use this trail today and another unit is firing over their heads."

The officer I spoke with asked where the troops were and I told him a lieutenant was bringing them to the barracks, and as far as I knew no one was injured.

If a 105 mm Howitzer had misfired, a lot of trainees could have been killed or injured. We certainly didn't want anything like friendly fire occurring on the base. It was the only time I came across a problem like that.

The troops were indeed okay. The lieutenant should have known better than to leave his troops in harm's way.

A few days later, our colonel talked to the other colonels from numerous regiments about having a bowling tournament. As they agreed, other units heard about the tournament and jumped in also, so we had something going. We set up a round robin program where every team bowled against each team, and the top two teams would bowl for the championship of Fort Sill.

At the end of the round robin matches, the 6th and 7th Regiments were the top two teams and bowled for the Fort Sill Championship with our Regimental team winning by 116 pins. We had a very happy colonel.

I appreciated the opportunity to bowl for the US Army, and any time I wanted a three-day pass to bowl in a tournament the captain would write one out for me. However, when I wanted a pass to be with a certain young lady for the weekend, the captain would look at me and say, "You'll only get yourself in trouble, so forget it." I really didn't appreciate that kind of thinking, but couldn't do much about it.

***

During a weekend in the spring of 1945, the bowling alley owner, a young lady that worked for him, and I went to a bowling tournament about 150 miles away. After bowling in the tournament, of which we didn't have any success in, we started our drive back home. It was too late to get to Camp, so we stopped at an old hotel in a small town for the night.

As I got in my room and turned to lock the door, all I saw was a hook and eye lock. I had about

$150.00 in my wallet, and I didn't know what to do with it.

Looking around, I didn't see anywhere safe I could put it while I slept. Then, I spotted the window shade.

I pulled the shade down, turned off the light, took the money and rolled the shade back up with the money rolled up inside it.

Afterwards, I often thought about what people would have been thinking if the place caught on fire and I came running out holding on to a window shade.

Thankfully, nothing happened and we got on our way in the morning.

***

It was mid-summer before I was notified I was to be shipped out to the Presidio of Monterey, California to go to the Pacific Theater of War. It was a long train ride, down through the bottom of the Grand Canyon and through the mountains to California. I wasn't scared, just anxious to do my job, whatever that may be. As we were from different units. We had no idea where we were going to end up at overseas.

A few of us started a 25c-50c poker game during the train ride. We had a rule that if anyone had to pull KP duty or leave for any reasonable reason, they could come back into the game after a deal ended, and the person who replaced him had to step out.

When I was out of the game for a while, I talked to one of the train crew who told me there would be a stop at a division point to change crews. There was a general store there where we could buy things.

So, I was ready to jump off when we stopped, and the store was right in front of me. I was the first to get in and grab my wares before a group followed behind. Everyone was trying to pay so they could get back on the train as quickly as possible. I couldn't get near the counter to pay. Eventually I did, and was the last one out. I had to run to the train as I heard the engineer blowing the whistle to start moving. Thank God I made it, or I would have been stranded and really been in trouble.

It seemed they used every railroad between Fort Sill and the Presidio of Monterey, the trip took so long. When we finally arrived, I had won about $10.00 in the poker game, so I was happy. It wasn't a lot of money, but it was better than losing it.

I was unaware when I was on the troop train to Monterey that my mother had told Ardyth and Bob I was going overseas. Bob and Ardyth lived in Holtville, California, as he was stationed at a nearby naval base after he had returned from assignment overseas. He requested furlough time so they could come up to Monterey to meet me.

76

Our train was delayed, and not knowing when we would arrive, they stayed in their hotel room for several days. Each day Bob would go to the Army base to see if I had arrived yet.

When we finally did arrive I was notified about Bob and Ardyth waiting to see me, so I got a pass to go to town to see them at their hotel. We were only able to visit for a few hours before they had to head back to Holtville. Still, a short time was better than no time, and I was glad for the visit.

We were put in large 10-man tents to stay until we shipped out. We didn't have anything to do, but we could go to town. I took advantage of it and noticed there was a nice, not too large, bowling alley near the base.

A couple of days later we were sitting around in the tent when a soldier walked in, and asked for Meintzer.

I replied, "I'm Meintzer."

He replied, "Get your gear, you're being transferred to the Military Police Detachment here."

I said good bye to the men and went with the soldier. He told me where the barracks were and to report to the corporal of the guard.

At the MP barracks, I was issued my equipment, a side arm which was a .45 caliber automatic, an MP arm band and a baton. My first job was to direct traffic at an intersection in town, meanwhile the troops I was to go overseas with walked down to the ships to leave. I never found out why I was singled out and transferred to the MP Detachment. I had several incidents while serving as an MP. I was on duty at the main gate one morning as an old car drove up with the driver's window open.

I stuck my head in, asking, "What's your destination?" Then I saw the silver star on the man's collar.

I got my head out of the car fast, stood at attention, saluting, and said, "Have a good day, General.

He smiled at me, and said "At ease, soldier." Then he drove on.

After that instance, any time I was on duty at the main gate and saw his car coming I was at attention with a sharp salute.

Being near the coast, we had a lot of mornings when it was so foggy it was difficult to see any distance at all. The weather was different than what we had at Fort Sill, Oklahoma, or at home in Illinois.

It was the military police detachment's duty to raise the colors (the US flag) at the Post Headquarters every morning and retire them at days' end. One morning, another fellow and I were told to raise the colors so we took the flags over to post headquarters, untied the lanyard and pulled it down so we could clip the flag on the lanyard and raise the colors until it stopped, saluted, and returned to the guard house.

About an hour later a call came in from the general's office asking, "Who died?"

The corporal of the guard replied, "We haven't heard that anyone had died."

Through the phone I could hear a gruff voice say, "Then, why are the colors at half-mast?"

When he and I went outside, we saw the flag was indeed not at the top of the flag pole. We lowered the colors, removed it from the lanyard, and clipped it to the two top clips that we hadn't seen earlier and raised the colors to the top, saluted, and returned to the guard house with a sigh. That never happened again as long as I was taking care of the raising of the flag.

***

While I was on duty at the main gate one night I had a ball watching this one lieutenant. About a half block from the main gate was a house of ill repute with a couple of windows on the side of it that faced the main entrance to the Camp. I could see people walking up or down the stairs of the house. On the other side of the main gate was a dispensary that handled first aid problems.

I saw this lieutenant come down the stairs, out the door, running towards us and into the dispensary. A short time later, he was out of the dispensary and running towards the house and up the stairs. He made this round trip three times, and on the last trip, I thought of telling him to walk so he would save his energy for another trip. My mind was functioning for a change, so I kept my mouth shut. It made me wonder though what was wrong with his.

***

As MPs, one problem we had was going to the mess hall to eat our meals. Army regulations at the time were if you were wearing a side arm your head had to be covered, either by wearing a cap or helmet. While we were on duty, we always had to wear a side arm.

The captain in charge of the mess hall was a stickler on not wearing a head covering in her mess hall. (I don't blame her; Neva and I never cared for seeing men sitting at a table wearing a cap or hat. We feel it's disrespectful to those sitting with him.) We would explain to the captain we were on duty and couldn't remove our hats/helmets. Finally, she called our commanding officer about it and he advised her she had to feed us whether our heads were covered or not.

One thing I noticed while I was with the MP detachment was that we didn't have to patrol in the town, which was different than all the other camps I was stationed at for military duty. We had to direct traffic when ships were being loaded, but never patrol.

***

One day while I was in the guard house an MP at one of the exit gates called in, saying he was having a problem with some GIs. The corporal of the guard said, "Meintzer, get out there and straighten it out."

I jumped in a jeep, drove over to the gate, and there stood three GIs, thinking it was funny giving an MP a hard time.

I asked the three of them if they had permission to leave their post, and if so, I wanted to see it. They showed me their passes and I told them what they were doing would only get them in trouble and they better get moving. Just plain foolish. (In my opinion, the guard should not have been an MP as he was a person that got excited too quickly and his reactions could have caused more trouble.)

***

Periodically, we would have time off-duty to do what we wanted. (If you have ever read the book, *Cannery Row* by John Steinbeck, you might know what I'm referring to. The book was good; my experience was not so good.)

Cannery Row was about two blocks from the main gate of the Presidio of Monterrey. I walked over to the factory and asked if there was any chance of me getting g a job to pick up some extra money. I was advised I could work on the cannery line.

I had to cut off the head and gut the fish, but the fish were coming so fast up the line I couldn't keep up the "cutting and gutting" of them. Some went into the cans without being cleaned, I'm sorry to say.

By noon, I went to the office and told them I had to quit. They offered to pay me for my time, but I told them no, the experience working there was worth more than the money. That was seventy-one years ago and I have never knowingly eaten any canned fish in all those years.

When I was assigned to the MP detachment at the Presidio, I called home and told Mother to send me my bowling ball and shoes. She did, and on off-time I'd go to the bowling alley and practice.

One day while I was practicing, I noticed a fellow watching me. After a while, he came down and asked to get acquainted. He mentioned it looked like I knew my way around a bowling alley. I said, "Yes, I've been in a lot of them."

He asked me what my average game was.

I explained that being in the army for over a year hadn't allowed me to bowl in a league, so I didn't have an ABC average. I didn't want to mention anything about the Oklahoma Times tournament or the championship I played in at Fort Sill.

He asked if I would be willing to bowl on the team he sponsored in a league.

I said I would be glad to, but it was possible I would draw duty time that would make me miss a night without notice.

He said he understood, and that it would be okay. He put me down as a 150 average. I should have said, no. Show me with at least at an180 average, but I kept my mouth shut. BIG MISTAKE.

The first night of bowling, I scored 246, 201, and 237 for a 684 series. In the middle game of 201, I had two strikes. On the next shot, I bowled a strike, but I fouled. Then I had a 6-pin count on my second ball. If I hadn't fouled, I would have had over a 700 series.

The team sponsor and I went into the restaurant for a drink when a fellow who had been bowling on a team several alleys away from us came in and grabbed me by the arm, madder than hell. He complained about my coming into the league at a 150 average and then bowling a 684 series, a 228 average.

I found out later why he was really mad. For the past three years, he had held the high score in the league with a 683 score. I beat him out by 1 pin the first night of the season. The second night of bowling I scored 203, 220 and 230, for a 653 series.

Unfortunately, I wasn't able to stay in the league very long. A few weeks later, I was transferred back to Fort Sill, Oklahoma, where I was reassigned to the 7th Field Artillery Training Regiment. I worked in the S-3 section again, and on February 8, 1946, I was promoted to Tec 5 rank.

A while after that, I was transferred to Fort Knox, Kentucky and assigned to S-3 work at the Headquarters Company of the 3rd training regiment, in the Armored Cavalry. On April 19th, 1946, I was promoted to Sergeant. Then, on April 27, 1946, I was given orders to proceed to Fort Sheridan, Illinois, for discharge.

There was talk about a possible war with Russia. There was a push on getting veterans to sign up for the inactive reserve when they were discharged. I was thinking about it, as I was twenty years old, single, and had a rank of sergeant. If there was another war, I would be one of the first to go back into service. If I re-enlisted, I would keep my rank of sergeant. If I didn't, I would still be called into service and go back with no rank at all, starting at the bottom again. So, I enlisted in the reserve.

After I arrived at Fort Sheridan, Illinois and in the process of being examined before my discharge, the medical officer made a comment. "Sergeant, you have a sore throat. I know you want to go home as bad as I do, so I'll just make a note of it." And he approved the discharge.

84

I said, "Thank you, sir. It's not killing me."

I was home within the week, however I didn't know what was going to happen in the next ten days.

Knowing I was getting discharged, I applied to Bradley University in Peoria, Illinois to attend their engineering school. As soon as I received my discharge papers and got home, I asked Dad if I could use the car so I could register for school in the fall, not knowing I would never get there.

I was home for a few days when I started to feel sick. School would be put off indefinitely.

Neva and Gail Meintzer, June 21, 1947,
on their wedding day

Neva and Gail Meintzer on their honeymoon in Pike's Peak, CO, 1947

Chapter 5

One Sunday morning, Mother and Dad talked about a visit to see Grandma Moeller. I said I'd like to go along, as I hadn't seen her in over two years.

After we visited, we were returning home when Dad said, "Let's bowl a few games."

So we stopped in at the bowling alley. Mother and Dad liked to bowl and they each had a fair game average in the leagues they bowled in.

After the second game I said, "I don't feel very good. I'm sitting out the third game." So, Mother and Dad finished out their third game and we headed for home.

The following morning, I woke up feeling great—until I jumped out of bed, only to fall onto the bed on my back, not able to breathe either standing or lying flat in the bed. I had to be bent at the waist in order to breathe. I managed to dress myself and get downstairs.

"There's something wrong with me," I told Dad. So, he drove me over to the local doctor in town.

The doctor checked me over, made a note on my chart, then asked, "Didn't you just come home from the military?"

"Yes," I replied, "I was discharged a few days ago."

"Hmm…" the doctor said. "Rather than go any further in my diagnosis, I'll write a note for you to go to the veterans hospital in Heinz, Illinois."

He believed my illness had started while I was still in the Army, and therefore it should be taken care of by the Veterans Administration.

Dad and I went home to wait for Mother to come home from work so she could go with us. The pains in my chest were more severe now and I told Dad I couldn't wait any longer for her, the pain was getting too bad.

He said, "Okay, we'll leave right away."

We went out to the car and just as we were pulling out of the driveway, Mother was brought home by a co-worker. She went from their car to Dad's car, and we headed for Heinz Veterans Hospital.

When we arrived at the hospital, I told Dad to leave me at the front entrance so he could park the car and then come in to find me. I believe Mom stayed with him, since I don't recall her being next to me as I pulled myself up the stairs to the front door using the hand rails.

I didn't see anyone in the foyer, so I started down a long hallway hoping to find someone to help me, bent over as I was and walking very slowly.

When I was down about one-third of the way, a nurse crossed the hallway, looked up and saw me. She came running. She grabbed hold of me saying, "You need help."

She helped me get to the first examining room, and even though there were people waiting, she took me in ahead of them. She told a doctor how bad I was hurting and to check me out right away.

They examined me and took me to another floor to a room with three other men that had been there since World War I. I was twenty years old and not a person who prayed a lot, but I started praying that day that I would die as quick as possible the pain was so bad.

The next morning nine different doctors examined me, the first eight doctors asked me if I had any pain in my knees, hips, shoulders, elbows, or wrists. Each time I responded, "No, only in my chest and if I'm not bent over, I can't breathe."

And then the ninth doctor walked in.

He was huge and built like a brick out house, or a linebacker on a professional football team. He sure didn't look like a doctor to me and he wasn't wearing a white coat like all the rest of them were.

IIc asked me where I hurt and checked me over, turned to the other doctors and said, "Treat him with Sulfa for Rheumatic Fever with effusion (fluid from an organ in a cavity)," and walked out.

I never saw him again, but apparently all of the doctors respected him and followed his instructions.

While I was lying in bed, I was visited by people from the Salvation Army and the Red Cross, asking if there was anything I needed, such as tooth brushes, tooth paste, combs, etc. The Salvation Army gave military men the items, but if we got it from the Red Cross we had to pay for it.

A couple days after being treated, my doctor came in and told me I should have asked for one of the representatives from a service organization to file a claim against the US Army. I said, "But I wasn't shot or injured. I was sick."

He told me that sickness is no different than an injury, and figuring I wasn't going to do anything about it, he did it himself. A fellow from one of the service organizations showed up the next day, asking a lot of questions about what happened and said he would file a claim for me.

(I found out later the Department of Veteran Affairs awarded me a 100% disability and they would start paying me once I was discharged from the veterans hospital. It amounted to $137.00 per month which was a lot of money back in 1946.)

I still felt severe pains in my chest, and hoped I

would die so I wouldn't feel the pain. A nurse came in with a wheel chair, saying she had to take me to another place to have a treatment done.

At first neither one of us realized it, but after talking for a while as she was pushing me down the hallways, it dawned on us that we knew each other by name, as she also lived in Deerfield. We made this trip about two times a week, and each time she would turn to the left as we exited the room I was in.

After making the trip several times, I asked her why she didn't turn to the right now and then so I could see whatever was in the hallways that way. With the building being square, we would end up at the same place regardless of which way we left my room.

She insisted I didn't want to go that way.

After my asking several times, she finally agreed. "All right, but you aren't going to like it."

Boy, was she ever right. The first ward we had to go through had men from World War I in it. They hung in baskets hanging from the ceiling. I found out these were men badly gassed during that war and had been there ever since. It was so painful for them to lie on a bed, the only relief they had was to be hung that way. (It was a horrible scene and one that has stayed with me to this day.)

We never went that way again.

I was slowly getting better. Mother and Dad would

visit on the weekends, as they worked during the week, to find out how I was feeling. I was getting stronger and looking forward to getting out of the hospital.

Early during the war, the government passed a law that anyone drafted into the military, if and when they returned to it, would get their job back when they returned from serving. There were three of us that had the job I had and I was the third man to leave, so I didn't have much chance of getting my job back.

As I didn't know if the other two fellows returned while I was in the hospital, I wrote to the railroad to request my job back. I received a letter advising me that one of the fellows had claimed the job under the law, and it was his.

So knowing I had no job to return to, I focused all my energy on getting better so I could look for a new job once I was out of the hospital.

The time finally came when my doctor declared me healthy and fit enough to be discharged. I was told I couldn't lift anything over 40 pounds, to take it easy, and not go to work for a year.

I was advised to go to the pharmacy and pick up my prescription before going home. The pharmacy gave me a large mason jar of Sulfa tablets and told me to take them three times a day with plenty of water. Furthermore, after I was done with this jar to come back and get another jar of the pills at no cost to me.

I returned for the second jar, but never went back for another refill as I was afraid I would become immune to the pills. I don't know if I did the right thing not taking any more Sulfa tablets, but I didn't get a reoccurrence of Rheumatic Fever.

I was home for a while, however it was getting to me just sitting around. I took a trip out to Portland, Oregon to see a friend who was married and living there after he returned from serving his time in the military.

By the time I got home, I knew I had to do something or I'd go nuts sitting around doing nothing. Previously, I was always doing something, as I was accustomed to keeping busy. After a few more days at home, one of my army buddies mentioned he was working for the Milwaukee Road in the General Agents office in the Freight Department on Dearborn Street in Chicago. Since someone was getting transferred, he was getting a promotion to the next job, and they were looking for a replacement. He advised me to apply for the job. It was an office boys' position in the office.

I thought about it and there wasn't much else available for jobs. What did I have to lose? So, the next day I went down to the office and my friend took me into the boss's office and introduced me to his boss.

The man asked if I had served in the military,

and I responded I had. He then asked if I would take advantage of the schooling opportunity the government offered.

I said I would.

He told me I should go over to the College of Advance Traffic on Jackson Boulevard and sign up for their course. Then, come back to his office with the approval papers and he'd hire me to begin working tomorrow morning at 8 a.m.

I had no idea what I was getting into or about what the college taught. Still, I went over to the college and asked to sign up for their course. I said I was getting a job the next day with hours starting at 8 a.m. until 5 p.m.

The man that helped me with enrollment said that was okay and I could enroll in their night course, which was two nights a week for two years. So, I signed up and went back to the office and my new boss hired me. I never realized what was in store for me, or what opportunities would be available to consider. It was very different work from any railroad work I had done before.

My first day on the job my friend was going to assist and go with me to the Union Station where the General Offices of the Milwaukee Railroad was located. The company's post office was on the second floor and it was the first stop on both trips we would make, one in the morning and another in the afternoon.

Having worked in the Union Station prior to World War II, it wasn't difficult to find my way around. He introduced me to some people I didn't know from the Traffic Department, which didn't work closely with the Office of the Auditor of Expenditures and Joint Facilities Accounts.

We went to the mail room and a few of the fellows I knew from working there before said it was great seeing me back. We dropped off our outbound mail, picked up our inbound mail, and were ready to leave to return to our office.

As we stepped into the hall and turned to the north heading for the Adams Street elevators, I heard a woman calling my name.

I turned around to see who it was and saw Neva running towards us. "It's so nice to see you're back, Gail," she said.

We talked for a few minutes before we exited the building. On the way back to our office I said, "Boy, if Neva can remember me after two years, I think I'll ask her for a date."

My friend replied, "Forget it. You're wasting your time. When I came back, I asked her for a date and she wouldn't go out with me. She sure as hell won't go out with you."

I thought, who needs enemies with friends like that?

His comment didn't make me give up the idea, though. With the war ended, I couldn't buy a new or used car yet as the car companies were still switching from building war machines to retooling their companies to building cars again. When I got home, I asked Dad if I could use the car as I had a date on Saturday night with a woman living in Elgin, Illinois. (I had to be sure I could use the car before asking for a date.)

Dad said, "Saturday's September 27th, our 44th wedding anniversary."

Then Mother said, "Chris, let Bud have the car. We're not going anywhere."

So Dad conceded and gave his permission.

Yippee! Now that I had the car, the next day on my first trip to Union Station, I saw Neva and asked her for a date on Saturday night.

"I'll let you know tomorrow," she said.

The next day I saw Neva again on the first trip over to the building and she said, "Yes, I'll be happy to go out with you on Saturday night."

I asked for her address and I was right—the best way to get there was by car. I had never been to Elgin before, but I wasn't nervous. She gave me good directions. (By the way, in dating Neva, I had to go through a Traffic Circle or "Roundabout" each way every time I traveled to Elgin. This was back in 1946 and 1947. I mention that simply to let people know that these roundabouts we now have in Wisconsin and elsewhere are not a new thing.)

On Saturday, I drove out and following her

instructions, I had no trouble getting to her parents' house. I knocked and Neva opened the door. As I was coming in, I noticed her mother and dad, along with a younger girl who I assumed was her sister. I shook hands with her father when she introduced me and greeted her mother and sister.

Then we left and enjoyed a movie downtown. We stopped and had something to eat, then drove back to her parents' home. We sat in the car in the driveway and talked for a long time. I told her that Dad had let me have the car even though it was his and Mother's 44th wedding anniversary. We commented about two people living together that long. (Never realizing, of course, that in the future, we would get married and much later in life celebrate our 69th anniversary in June, 2016.)

After this first date, neither of us ever dated anyone else. One thing we did do on all of our dates was talk about anything and everything, getting to know each other. We even talked about what we would do if something happened with our parents.

One night when I was at our bowling alley, a good friend who was a train engineer on the Milwaukee Road said, "I understand you're dating Charlie Jewell's daughter."

I looked at him and asked, "How the hell did you know that?"

He laughed and said, "Charlie's asking all of us about what kind of a man you are. We didn't leave anything out when we told him how bad you are."

I knew he was pulling my leg about how bad I was, but the fact Neva's dad was checking on me was a shock.

We also "necked" in the car on dates, so we weren't any different than any of the other couples at that time. At work, when we would meet, we would go in the stair wells and neck. We got in our share of kissing and hugging.

There were some good elevator operators working, especially on the Adams Street side of the station. When young couples working on the railroads in the Union Station would get in the elevators, they would stop the car between floors and turn off the lights and say, "You have one to two minutes."

Then you heard, "The lights are coming back on," and they did. Those fellows were very obliging.

***

Periodically, Neva would spend a weekend at our place, using my bedroom, and I'd sleep on a cot in the sun room.

The first night she slept at the house she had the hell scared out of her. We lived about a half block from the Milwaukee Road mainline between Chicago and Milwaukee and both passenger and freight trains ran that route. We lived there long enough we never noticed, but for the first night she slept there she thought the train was coming through the house. The noise of the train pounding the ground does have an effect when you're not use to it.

I was still bowling a lot, and when Neva would spend a weekend at our place I would take her to the bowling alley in the afternoons trying to teach her how to bowl. It never worked, as everyone *not* bowling would sit behind us. They'd watch and talk about us, which made Neva so nervous she couldn't handle it. This was a big mistake on my part. I should have taken her to another bowling alley in a nearby town where I wasn't so well known.

I was bowling on a team that was sponsored by a restaurant, and we bowled almost every Saturday night against other teams for money. After we got done, we would go to the restaurant for dinner and a few drinks. (We never knew it then, but the cook at that restaurant would later teach Neva how to make authentic spaghetti sauce the Italian way.)

The restaurant, while it was illegal, had slot machines. So on the way out after dinner, I would get change for a dollar and play each machine once with a nickel, a dime, a quarter and a half dollar. If we won, I'd take the winner off and keep the rest of the money. By the time we got married, we had won enough money to buy a stove.

***

Neva's oldest brother came home from serving in the US Navy. He was at Pearl Harbor when the Japanese had their sneak attack on December 7th, 1941, and then went through the entire Pacific Theatre of war. Neva invited me to come over and meet him, and have dinner with the family as they were going to have steak.

I was a steak eater now and really enjoyed a rare-to-medium-rare steak. When her mother put the meat platter on the table the steak looked like pieces of shoe leather. Neva told me later that her dad liked his meat very well done. I knew I was going to have to teach Neva that steak should be eaten rare or medium rare.

Later on, we learned to eat raw ground round on rye bread with onions and salt and pepper. I also found out her dad liked his apple pie with beef gravy over it.

Our dating was going along very well, and I felt like we would make a good couple. So, when Valentine's Day was coming up, I thought it would be a good time to become engaged to be married. Besides the engagement ring, I also had a Valentine's Day gift for her.

I gave her the gift when I got to her house, and after going out for the evening, I gave her the ring while we were sitting in the car in the driveway. She accepted my proposal immediately.

Back in that time, with so many coming home

from the war, it was difficult finding places to live. Neva set the date—June 21, 1947—for the wedding, because her brother and his wife were moving out of the apartment they had, and we were lined up to get it.

We were going to get married in the Methodist Church in Elgin, Illinois at 4 p.m. The reception was to be held at Neva's parents' home. There were both families present and each of us had a few friends invited—a total of about forty people. Coffee, soft drinks, sandwiches, and cake were served. About 8 p.m., we left to stay in the Morrison Hotel in Chicago for our wedding night. Looking back, I don't think the wedding was more than $500.00 total and our marriage is still going strong sixty-nine years later. We got our money's worth.

Neva was a little upset before the wedding as I didn't get the right color flowers for the bouquets, but her dad told her it was all right and she was going to be married. I always got along good with her dad and mother.

The next day we were scheduled to take the Rock Island Railroad Train to Colorado Springs, Colorado in a bedroom suite in a Pullman Car. They were serving lunch in the dining car around noon, and at that time, the train was going through the state of Iowa. I got a shock when we were ordering our lunch in the dining car. I told the waiter we would like a drink. I was advised they couldn't serve liquor while the train was passing through the state of Iowa as the state didn't allow liquor to be sold.

It seemed it took forever to get through the state and into Nebraska. A few hours later, we had our drink when we had our dinner while we were traveling through Nebraska. We spent one night in the sleeper car before arriving in Colorado Springs.

While in Colorado Springs, I rented a car and we spent several days driving around, seeing as many of the sights as we could cram in during that time. We also went up to Pike's Peak, which was a lot of fun. Just can't get away from the railroads.

One night during our honeymoon we decided to splurge for dinner, so we went to a local hotel to eat. We ordered steaks and waited and waited, and by the time they came I had one taste and knew we would have been better off eating anywhere else, as it was terrible. I guess I should have known better when I saw there wasn't anyone else in the dining room.

There was a swimming pond near our hotel, so the day before we were to start back home, we went to the swimming pond. BIG MISTAKE! We didn't realize the difference the altitude made between Illinois and Colorado when you expose your body to the sun. I ended up with a severe case of sunburn. It was so bad we couldn't sleep in one bed. I had blisters all over my back and had to sleep on my stomach both in the hotel and in the sleeping car going back to Illinois.

The apartment we were going home to was more a hovel than anything else, but at least we had a place to live. We didn't stay there very long as Neva found us another place about five blocks away. This apartment was much better, and bigger. We were enjoying our marriage and being together every day. I was doing some bowling and got on a team at the local bowling alley, and other than work, that was the only time I spent away from her.

***

Christmas was coming up and we bought a large Christmas tree to put up. On Christmas day, we exchanged gifts. Neva gave me a leather bowling ball bag that I still have to this day. (I don't bowl anymore as I'm not too steady on my feet and afraid I'll fall.)

We were planning on spending the day together at home when we received a phone call from Neva's mother. She and her three sisters gathered at the home of one sister who lived in Rockford, Illinois every Christmas for dinner. Neva's dad had to work that day on the railroad, as he was a train engineer, so they asked me to drive the family to Rockford.

I said, no, as the roads were very icy. He didn't have insurance on the car, and as I have never driven the car before, I was leery as to how it would handle on those icy roads. I asked why either of the sons didn't offer to drive, and her mother said they had made other plans.

I finally agreed to drive, and we went over to their house and headed to Rockford, about 40 miles away. I was traveling about 35 miles per hour, due to the icy roads when Neva said, "Can't you go a little faster? We won't get there for dinner."

I stepped on the gas pedal a little harder, and the next thing I knew the car was sliding sideways across the road towards the ditch. The car flipped over one-and-three quarter times before it stopped on its side with the driver's side door facing the sky.

I asked if everyone was okay. They replied, yes they were, so I said we have to get out of the car. I climbed through the window, but we had a hard time getting Neva's mother out as she was so scared. Then, Neva and I got her sister out and I pulled Neva out last. I commented that we had to notify the police, and the only place that was open and had a phone was a nearby bar.

So, the four of us walked to the bar, leaving the car on its side in the ditch. I went into the bar and asked if I could use their phone to report an accident, and the bartender handed me their phone.

The police asked if anyone was injured and when I told them no, they advised they wouldn't send an officer out due to the road conditions.

Neva's mother thought bars were terrible places to go and was giving Neva a hard time as Neva tried to get her to go inside in order for them to get out of the cold. Finally, Neva slapped her in the face to get her in the bar. That's when her mother found out it wasn't as bad as she thought.

We called Neva's mother's sister, and told them where we were. She sent one of the men out to pick us up and bring us back to the house so we could have dinner. When dinner was over, we went home with other family members.

When her dad came home that night from work, we told him what happened. He said, "We'll go back there tomorrow and see if we can get the car back home."

The next day, Neva's dad, her two brothers and I went back to where the accident happened. We tipped the car over so it was on all four wheels, and when he tried the ignition it started. So he drove it home and I told him we would buy it from him as I damaged it. It cost me $300.00 to buy it.

Since the roof was caved in, I got a hacksaw and sawed off the top of the car. We now had a "Roadster" for the spring, summer and fall. We always kept a couple of umbrellas in the car in case it rained while we were driving. It got us around, and we had fun going on one day or two day trips.

At the end of summer, I took the car over to my parents' house and got to work taking the car body off the chassis. My dad and I went to a scrap yard and found another body that would fit the chassis and had it trucked to Dad's place.

With some assistance from the neighbors, we lifted off the old body and put on the new one I bought, and then I spent several days hooking up everything. It was a good idea I took a course on Auto Mechanics in high school, although I never realized at the time I would use the knowledge in this manner. We used the car through winter and it worked fine.

While we were at my parents' home working on the car, the restaurant I used to bowl for now had a trailer park behind the restaurant. They told us there was a couple interested in selling their trailer. We checked it out and decided to buy it.

We moved in, and I started bowling on their team again. Our trailer was the closest one to the restaurant, and I often went in through the kitchen to the bar. The Italian woman who was the chef there was a friend of my mother's, so when she found out who Neva and I were, she told Neva she would teach her how to cook some Italian dishes. She did an excellent job teaching Neva how to cook them.

***

From the time we came back from our honeymoon until now—it was 1949 at this point in my life—I received a number of promotions in the clerical jobs and was now the Tracing clerk. It was a position that had me finding the location of freight cars when customers wanted to know where their cars were so they would know when to expect them to arrive.

Neva and I had been trying for a long time to have a child and weren't having any luck. Neva finally decided we should see a doctor about the issue. When we went to see him, I told him what had happened to me in grammar school when I got kicked, but he said, "No, I usually find the problem is with the woman."

He told us that when Neva finished with her time of the month we were to have sexual intercourse every day for a minimum of ten days. If nothing happened the first month, we were to continue the next month, and continue each month until she became pregnant.

When I heard him say this, I thought I died and gone to heaven, no excuses, sex every day, by doctor's orders. Again, I didn't know what I was getting into.

The first month went by and we started on the second month. The second month went by and we started on the third month. That one went by, and we started on the fourth month. During the ten day span I was getting tired.

One night I was getting ready for bed, and Neva commented, "Remember we're in the ten day span, so I'll be right with you."

I told Neva when the doctor had told us what we had to do, I thought I had died and gone to heaven. I found out I had gone to purgatory instead, and this was turning out to be a hard job. "Why can't we forget about tonight and we'll do it tomorrow," I said. That didn't go over well with Neva, so I was really tired that night. Thank God, it finally worked and Neva got pregnant.

***

Neva's father worked for the Milwaukee Railroad. There is an old adage saying in a large crowd of people, if there are two railroad men they will find each other. That's because they will be talking about railroading for hours.

This is something that was causing a little problem for Neva, as every time we would be visiting her parents and both or one of her brothers were present, her dad would start talking about the railroad. I'd join in on the conversation, but her dad and I would be talking, and her brothers were left sitting there saying nothing, as they did other work elsewhere and didn't know what we were talking about.

On the way home, Neva would complain to me

that I should let her brothers talk once in a while, so what could I do. I was trying to get "Brownie Points" with her father that first night, and I reacted like a railroad man would, but we lived through it.

***

It was summer and we decided to take a vacation with Neva's older brother and his wife in Minong, Wisconsin, not realizing what was going to be at our home when we got back. When the week ended her brother and his wife went home, and Neva and I continued to Winnipeg, Canada to visit our Milwaukee Road office there.

After an uneventful visit in Winnipeg, we started home, but when we arrived, I got a big surprise that indicated I was already *late* to report for my physical for the US Army.

I reported for my physical the next day and then went to work to show my boss my orders. He called the vice president of our department, telling him what happened. The vice president wrote a letter to the US Army explaining the important job I had with the Milwaukee Railroad working on the war effort.

The letter worked the first time and I received a 30-day delay, but the second time, they wrote back to the vice president and told them the US Army needed me more than the railroad did for the

Korean War effort, and I was to report to Fort Riley, Kansas by November 10, 1950.

After arriving at Fort Riley, Kansas and receiving my clothing supplies, I was ordered to go to Fort Leonard Wood, Missouri. That fort wasn't quite as organized while I was there. I was assigned to Battalion Headquarters as the Operation Sergeant. It was difficult doing a good job when I didn't have the right equipment available. There were a lot of trucks on the base, but they were owned by the Missouri National guard, and Army personnel couldn't use them. At one point, it was necessary for me to move high explosive rockets in my personal car from where the ammo was stored to the firing range for our recruits.

As Neva was pregnant with our first child when I received my orders, she moved into her folk's home to stay until it was almost time to deliver the baby. Then she moved into my folk's home. When my parents thought it was time, they contacted the Red Cross to get me leave time to come home for the birth of the baby. I had a 10-day leave, so every night for the first nine days, I would back the car into the garage so we could get out fast to head for the hospital in Highland Park. But nothing happened.

On the tenth night, I parked the car in the garage engine first, and sure enough, Neva woke me up saying we had to go to the hospital. Just as we got to the hospital in Highland Park, I was getting her out of the front seat of the car when her water broke. Neva was in labor for a very long time before our daughter, Pamela Ann, arrived.

The Red Cross got me an extension on my leave so I could stay and take them back to her folk's home. Neva and the baby stayed in the hospital for ten days, and our total bill was $75.00. (I imagine a lot of people would like a bill like that when they have children now.) As soon as the two of them were settled in at her parents' home, I left to go to camp.

It wasn't long after I returned to camp that we were hearing rumors that a group of us were going to be sent to Indiantown Gap Military Reservation in Pennsylvania. The orders finally came down, and a few other men and I were to report there by March 5, 1951.

When I arrived in Lebanon, Pennsylvania, which is close to the Reservation, I stopped in at the bar and grill in the local hotel. While I was there, I got to know the owner, which later helped when Neva and the baby moved out to Pennsylvania to live with me.

When I reported to camp, I was assigned to a battalion as Operation Sergeant, and found out the Operation Sergeant at our Regimental Headquarters was a friend of mine from the Milwaukee Road, which made it easier for us to accomplish our jobs.

We had all of the equipment and area's we needed to do our jobs, but one thing can screw up anything, and that one thing were the recruits we received to train. The first group of recruits came from the eastern coastal states.

We set up the training schedules so the Company commanders, officers, and NCOs (non-commissioned officers) could start training them. We had a good group of captains, first lieutenants, and second lieutenants to work with—all veterans from World War II.

My job as Operation Sergeant was such that I only worked with officers, not the NCOs like the sergeants and corporals did. The officers I worked with were more interested in getting the job done and working as a team, than worrying about military etiquette, so there were eyes raised at times when I was talking with them.

One day a captain from "A" Company came in shaking his head. One of his recruits had told the captain that he needed to go home as he owed some money, and the people he owed told him if he didn't come home to pay them immediately they would come to camp and get him. The kid was scared to death. The captain told him they were not going to come and touch him; he was in the US Army now and no one would be able to bother him.

It was bound to happen and it happened to me, too. I was working at my desk on the weekly training schedule when I heard a voice say, "Sergeant, I need to talk with you."

I nodded and said, "Okay, I'll be right with you," not looking up to see who was there.

The next thing I heard was the man saying, "Sergeant, don't you know military etiquette?"

With that, I stood up at attention, turned and looked at a second lieutenant. I said, "Sorry Sir, what can I do for you?"

He continued to chew me out before he left, never saying what he wanted to say to me. Never seeing him before, I knew he must have just received his commission from OCS (Officers Candidate School).

The ribbing I received from the warrant officer, and the other NCOs in the office was incredulous. Even the battalion commander and my boss, both captains, came out of their offices and laughed. "Well, it looks like we'll have to send Sergeant Meintzer to school to learn *military etiquette*."

All I could do was sit and take it, but in my head I was already figuring out what I could do to run his ass from one end of camp to the other end, and back again, a couple of times a day. There wouldn't be any way anyone could make a complaint.

I went home thinking about the embarrassment I was feeling, and what I could do to fix things. I always came up with the same thing—if I do anything like what I wanted to do, the NCOs and recruits would pay the same penalty as he would. I couldn't do that to them.

The next morning as I was working at my desk I heard a "Hey, Sarge," and I immediately stood at attention and turned to see who it was. It was a first lieutenant who was a really good officer I worked closely with. He was interested in all of us working as a team.

He said, "Forget it, we're a team and don't need all the BS."

Then he went on to say, "Last night I heard about the incident that occurred between a certain second lieutenant and you, and I saw to it that it won't happen again. If it does, you get hold of me and I'll straighten that bastard out for good. And, don't you do what I know you're thinking. You can't penalize the recruits and NCOs to get to him."

He was right and I knew it. "I was thinking about it, but it would just punish the NCOs and recruits, and they don't deserve it."

There was never another incident with that second lieutenant. In fact, I never recalled his coming into Battalion Headquarters again. At the time, I thought it was amazing that the first lieutenant had the same thoughts that I was going to make it really tough on that second lieutenant. However, we had worked together for a while and more or less knew what the other would do under different circumstances, so it wasn't that far-fetched. While the officers out-ranked us, operation sergeants were the ones who drew up the training schedules as to what the officers would do with the recruits every hour of the day from 7 a.m. to 5 p.m., and where it would be done.

Normally there was a good working relationship between us, as it made our work more easy for all of us. Whereas, if there were hard feelings between an officer and an operation sergeant for some reason, we could arrange his schedule where he would have his training areas all over the camp, as compared to having them close together so there wasn't a lot of time spent running from one place to another.

We were having some serious situations throughout the camp on weekends with some of our recruits that came from the eastern coastal states. What happened was due to a state highway running through the reservation, and the US Army personnel couldn't stop people from driving on that road through the reservation. If I hadn't seen it myself, I wouldn't have believed it. Parents driving over to the Camp with their daughters, so their daughters could "make out" with their boyfriends in the back seat of the cars as they drove through the reservation, or they would try to park in out-of-the-way spots, like the back of the firing ranges or in the hospital parking lots.

Finally, it got so bad the commanding officer of the Camp put out an order that an officer and an NCO would ride together daily in an official US Army vehicle and check all vehicles parked anywhere within the confines of the military reservation, getting the name, rank and serial number to be reported to Post Headquarters. If there wasn't any military personnel in the car, they were to be escorted off the reservation.

One evening, I was with a second lieutenant driving around to see if any cars were suspicious. We found one in the Post Hospital parking lot. We knew there were people in the car as the windows had moisture on them. As we drove over to the car and since it was on my side, I said, "I'll check it out," and got out of the car with our car blocking the other car from moving.

When I knocked on the window of the driver's side, the front door opened so fast I had difficulty getting out of the way. I spotted his "Oak Leaf Cluster" showing he was a major. I saluted, and before I could say anything, the second lieutenant was standing at my side.

"Major, we're under orders from the commanding officer of the Post. We need your name, rank and serial number, as well as the young lady who is with you."

We found out that she worked in the hospital. I don't know what happened to them, but we did our job as ordered.

***

About every other week, I had to send a couple of NCOs to Fort George G. Meade in Maryland to go to the 2nd Army Discussion Leaders Course and return them back to Camp. It got to the point where I had sent every NCO from all of the companies in the battalion, so when the battalion commander asked me who I was sending next, I replied, "I've sent all of our NCOs, so there isn't anyone left to send."

He looked at me and said, "Have you gone yet?"

"No Sir, but I don't believe I need it."

"Put your name on the list." His response was not what I expected.

So I went to school on April 1, 1951 and returned on April 7, 1951, and at the time I wasn't happy about it. Now I know better, as I look back on my career with the railroad, that course taught me about public speaking, and I used the information learned there a lot later in my career with the Milwaukee Railroad.

***

Neva and the baby had come out to live with me, so I applied for separate rations to live "off Post" and be with them when I wasn't on duty. When they arrived, I had a room at a hotel in Pottstown,

Pennsylvania. Our baby had colic and kept most of the people up for a good part of the night, so the other tenants were not too happy with us. While we were there, we went over to the hotel in Lebanon, Pennsylvania where I knew the hotel owner, as I had spent many nights drinking scotch and water and talking with him. Then I'd head back to Camp.

When we walked in, I introduced him to Neva and the baby. He said, "Sarge, while you and your wife are eating, I'll hold the baby."

While we ate, he carried our baby up and down the sidewalks of the town, showing her to everyone he knew. We also met his wife and sister-in-law. They had a two-story house with the kitchen, living room and dining room downstairs, and upstairs were two bedrooms and the bathroom.

The next time we came in to eat, the owner, before we even sat down, asked us if we would like to move from the hotel in Pottstown. When we said yes, we would like to, he told us he had talked with his wife and sister-in-law, and they all agreed we could rent the downstairs of their house and use the bathroom upstairs.

We told him that would be fine and we would be happy to do it, but our baby cries a lot due to having colic. "Don't worry about that," he said, "I'd be happy to walk the baby anytime she cries."

So we moved in and stayed there as long as I was stationed at Indiantown Gap Military Reservation.

***

Several months passed before we received orders to report to the firing range to qualify on the M-1 Rifle, as most of us were going to be sent overseas soon. We were on the range firing when an officer drove up to the officer in charge of the range and told him to stop us from firing, as we were going to be sent home. This was one of the few times I wondered if they knew what they were doing.

When I arrived at the Battalion Headquarters I learned I would be going home on September 11, 1951. Neva and I packed up to leave, and the folks we were staying with were crying about our leaving. They were very nice people and we were sorry that we had to leave them, but we did want to return home to where our families lived.

As we arrived home a few days later, we found out we faced another hurtle we'd need to overcome. When I was called back into service for the Korean War, we had to sell our trailer and put the money into the MR credit union in Chicago. The people in charge of the credit union made a large number of bad loans, and the state of Illinois came in and closed the credit union.

We received about ten cents on the dollar for what we had in the credit union, so we lost almost all of the money we had saved. We didn't have enough money to rent a place to live. A friend had a house trailer stored at the trailer camp we used to live at, so we lived there for a while until we could save some money, as I was back working at the Milwaukee Railroad.

We finally found an apartment in Elgin, Illinois to live. One weekend morning we were eating breakfast on our card table, as we didn't have a table and chairs yet, and I was swearing because I spilt my coffee because the table was so wobbly. Just then, my mother and dad walked in.

Mother said, "What's going on that you have to swear like that, Gail?" Then she saw what happened and said, "Get your coats on. We're going to buy you a kitchen table and chairs." Thank God for my mother. There was no more spilt coffee or milk.

***

It was difficult living in that apartment as the owner wouldn't allow me to park my car in the parking areas or driveway, as he was running his business out of his house. I had to park it on the road in front of the house. One morning, I came out to go to town and found that someone had sideswiped my car. The police had him, but the kid's old man knew someone and the kid got off easy. However, I did get my car fixed.

After that, we found an apartment in Deerfield, Illinois with a garage and moved there. I became involved with the Amvets Organization. When it was getting close to New Year's Eve, the organization decided to have a New Year's eve party. It was $7.50 a person for all you can eat and drink, and dancing with a juke box playing. It was a good time and we had a lot of fun, plus the organization ended up with a small profit. In time, I became Commander of the Post.

At work, I was promoted from Carload Tracer to the Chicago Rate Clerk. This move took me out of the jobs governed by union rules, and I was now considered as one of the management personnel. In the 1950s, we didn't have to join the union, but had to work under union rules and received union wages. Shortly after my move to Chicago Rate Clerk, the company and union agreed to have a "closed shop" where everyone other than management personnel had to join the union in order to work.

The schooling I received at the College of Advance Traffic was now very beneficial in my job. I spoke with the assistant general agent in the office one day and he told me how when he was young, he would eat a couple of bags of peanuts. The smell of the peanuts would mask the smell of the liquor he had been drinking.

In July of 1953, I was transferred to Milwaukee, Wisconsin as a City Freight Agent. Before we moved to Milwaukee, I stayed at a hotel, and the fellow I would be replacing took me out to show me the territory I would work in. We met many of the customers.

My territory covered the Milwaukee Stockyards. I was talking with our agent there one day when we decided we'd have a cup of coffee, so on our way to the restaurant I saw the USDA inspector and asked him to join us. Boy, did that man ever jump on my neck about trying to bribe a government official.

I said I don't know how buying someone a cup of coffee is trying to bribe them, but if that's what he is thinking, forget it. I was just trying to be friendly and kept walking.

The next day the fellow I was replacing said we were taking a customer out for lunch. After the third martini, while the other two were talking, I told the bartender that if any more drinks were ordered to put water in my glass. We finally got away from the bar and sat down to eat lunch. It was 2:30 p.m. After we left, the customer went home and we found out later he ran into a tree adjacent to his driveway. I was dropped off at the hotel and the man training me went home to a mad wife when he walked in so intoxicated. I never ordered more than two drinks in front of a customer again.

I found an apartment to live in, and Neva and I arranged to move there. After a month and a half, we realized it was not a good place to live in, so we started to look for a different home. We found a nice first floor apartment on the southwest side of

Milwaukee. The apartment had been just built, and we told them we had some wallpaper in mind that we would like them to put in the kitchen, if they would. It was a railroad motif and they were happy to oblige. A win-win situation.

The assistant general agent in Chicago was transferred to Milwaukee and promoted to the general agent status. Shortly after, I came in to talk to him and he noticed the smell of peanuts. He looked at me and said, "I know I shouldn't have told you that story."

"No," I said, "I just like peanuts. I didn't have a drink today."

***

As I was a member of the Milwaukee Traffic club, we went to a dinner-dance the club held. Going through the buffet line, I saw a large platter of something and since I didn't know what it was, but most of the people were taking it with rye bread and onions, I asked the gentleman ahead of me if he did.

He replied, "It's raw ground round."

I passed on it, as there was a lot of other food that looked good.

The next time I saw my mother, I told her about the people I saw eating raw meat.

She said, "Oh, Bud, that's good. We served it at

the restaurant. At times, people would even request a raw egg to put on top of it."

It took me a long time before I could eat raw meat, but once I tasted it, I really enjoyed it. And ordered it many times after that first time. (We don't eat it any longer, as we don't know of any meat markets that can sell clean raw ground round. You do have to be careful where you buy it before eating it.)

There was also a restaurant in West Allis I loved to go to as they always put a basket of salted rye rolls on every table. The rolls were delicious, to the point where one night Neva and I took her sister and friend over there for dinner. I ate so many rye rolls I couldn't eat my dinner when it was served. (I've never seen them at any other restaurant since then, but being I'm not supposed to have salt anymore, it doesn't make a difference now. Boy, did I enjoy them!)

***

The top boss in the office loved to play golf and he always wanted to have me in his group, which I didn't appreciate, as I never enjoyed being that friendly with my boss. (The more you're with them, the more they notice any weaknesses you might have.)

One day, I had to play with them. It was about the third hole, a par four. My drive went in the rough and I completely missed my swing at the ball for my second shot. I swung again and put the ball on the green. I two putted, and he asked what I had for a score so I replied, "I had a five."

"No you didn't, you had a par four," he said.

I looked at him and said again, "I had five as a score."

He came back with another retort. "You had a four, a drive, in the rough, and then your second shot on the green, and two putts for a four."

I replied very firmly, "My drive went in the rough, I missed my second shot, I missed it completely, put my third shot on the green, and two putted for a five."

"I thought that was a practice swing."

To which I said, "It wasn't a practice swing. I was trying to hit the ball and it counts as a swing, so I had a five."

"I don't cheat when I'm playing golf." I held my tongue, but I certainly didn't want to. He never counted my swings or challenged my score for the rest of the day.

***

There were four of us that played golf almost every Saturday morning at one of Milwaukee County's golf courses on the city's southwest side. We would meet at the clubhouse at 4:45 a.m. for coffee and a donut, and then tee off at 5 a.m. If you shot over an 85, you found yourself paying everyone when we finished playing at 9 a.m. Afterwards, I went home to get a couple of hours of sleep. My ability to play golf and bowl helped me to get to know our business associates.

There was a bar not far from our railroad office that was called Dirty Helen's. It was run by a former madam of a house of ill repute, and the only drinks she served was beer or shots of hard liquor. If you ordered a martini or a Manhattan, she would tell you what she thought of someone who drank drinks like that. There were no stools at the bar or tables and chairs in the rest of the room. You either stood or sat on the floor.

The cliental ran from men in work clothes to men and women in nice dress clothes, and you were apt to run into a senator or other government official on occasion. The few times I was there I never saw any trouble or heard swearing. Everyone was respectful of the place, and of Helen.

***

Neva and I had been working on having another child, as it had been about four years since Pam was born. After going through the same situation that we went through to get our first child, Neva was finally pregnant again and the baby's birth was due to happen sometime in August of 1955.

After two and a half years in Milwaukee, the boss called me in and told me I was being transferred to Green Bay, Wisconsin and promoted to Traveling Freight Agent in July of 1955. As Neva's doctor did not want her to move until after the baby was born, I would leave on Monday morning for Green Bay, work all week, and return home to Milwaukee for the weekend.

After the first week in Green Bay, I came home and told Neva that I thought I was going to have a hard time working there, as I was asked a lot of questions by most of the customers, such as "What parish are you going to join?"

This was a shock to me as I'd never run into that before in my life. All of my dad's siblings married into the Catholic religion, and as he had eight brothers and sisters, I was aware of Catholicism, but not to the level of talking about it. I was also a staunch Chicago Bears fan which didn't help me any being in Packer territory—although in two years they "brain-washed" me, so I became a Packer fan and have remained one ever since.

When I was transferred, my boss told me not to sponsor a bowling team, as they had been sponsoring one before, in the Green Bay Traffic Club Bowling League. But after meeting a number of our customers and listening to them, I realized it would be a big mistake not to do this, so I had my wife sponsor the team. Here again, my ability on the bowling alley paid off. I was one of the highest average bowlers in the league and everyone knew me.

After the bowling league ended for the season and new officers were voted in for the following year, in 1956, I was voted in as secretary/treasurer of the league. I made friends with a large group from the trucking industry which helped me in becoming an officer in the Green Bay Traffic Club.

In 1957, I was voted in as director of the Green Bay Traffic Club. In 1958, I was voted in as secretary/ treasurer of the club, and in 1959 as the first vice president of the club. In 1960, I was voted in as president of the club.

The Traffic Club held its annual dinner in December of each year, and in 1959, the newly elected second vice president asked me to help him make the arrangements for the dinner. We were able to obtain Mr. Victor Riesel as our guest speaker.

Mr. Riesel was an American newspaper journalist and columnist who specialized in news related to labor unions. An acid attack in 1956, when a hired thug hurled acid in his face had left him permanently blind. He had his body guard and secretary with him at all times. We publicized the dinner meeting and had so many requests for tickets to attend that it overflowed the main ballroom of the Northland Hotel. We had to have tables put in the hallway to accommodate the demand for dinner. We had over

600 people in attendance.

When I was elected president of the Traffic Club, the railroad company promoted me to District Freight Agent. One day in 1956, the traffic manager of one of the largest paper mills in Green Bay called to ask to see me. I went over to meet him, and he told me he was a member of a team in the Green Bay Major League. He had a health problem and he would appreciate it if I would replace him on the team for the rest of the season.

I asked what night of the week they bowled on as it could have an effect on my traveling schedule to cover my territory. As it turned out to be a night I could work around, I said I would. There were eight weeks left in their season and I bowled 24 games, with the team ending with the second highest average in the league with a 192. The top average was 194.

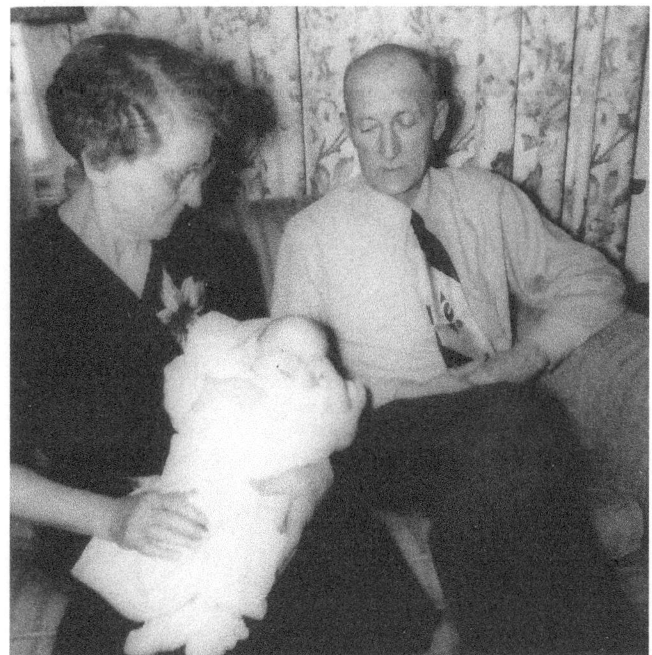

Minnie and Chris Meintzer with grandbaby in
early 1951

Chapter 6

In April of 1956, I made my first trip through my territory in the Upper Peninsula of Michigan. I left home on a Sunday evening and stopped in a motel in Iron Mountain, Michigan. I left there on Monday morning stopping in Crystal Falls first to see our agent there and then went on to Iron River to meet another agent.

Our agent in Iron River told me to turn around and drive back to Green Bay, as there was a bad snowstorm coming. I told him it was April and I wasn't worried about a snow storm. Boy, was I wrong.

I stopped in Watersmeet, Michigan to see the C & NW agent, but he wasn't in. The snow was already falling, so I thought I better keep going and got back on the highway heading for Ironwood.

It was difficult driving, but I did make it to

Ironwood. I was stuck there for three days due to the snow and the road conditions. When I was able to travel again I headed due south to get away from it and swore I would never go up there again until summer. It pays to listen to the local people.

***

The boss who I had the disagreement with on the golf course called me up one day and asked, "When you take customers out to lunch, where do you take them?"

I had no idea what he was talking about, and I said so.

"I'm looking at your expense account," he said, "and you show several times taking customers out for lunch but the report shows it costs only $5.00 each time. Where can you go and what are you buying them?"

Understanding what he was getting at, I said, "Look at the one on Friday. That was a bar and restaurant on Velp Avenue going north out of town. Martinis are fifty cents apiece, one each at the bar waiting for a table, that's one dollar. Two lobster tail salads, a dollar and a quarter each, that's two dollars and fifty cents. Each of us had another martini, another dollar, and a fifty cent tip. That's $5.00. The customers like to go there on Fridays."

He didn't object, so I went on to explain another

receipt. "The other place is in downtown Green Bay, drinks are the same price. This place specializes in prime rib sandwiches at a dollar and a quarter each. Again it's $5.00 for lunch. Customers like to go here during the week."

His reply was "I'm coming up during the week and I want to go to one of these places."

I said, "Okay, tell me when so I won't schedule a trip out of town."

He came up the next week and enjoyed a great lunch. He couldn't get over the prices and said, "You're making everyone else look foolish with these prices, so add more money to them."

I didn't want to cheat on my expense account, but he put me in a position where I had no choice.

I had another run-in with him and my immediate boss on my expense account. It happened after I was more familiar with my territory. I looked at my previous expense accounts and started comparing figures on staying overnight to driving back and forth. I found I could save money by driving compared to staying overnight.

The first month I started driving home, I had a call from both of them on the phone asking what I was doing when I sent my expense account in for that month. Neither one of them would listen to my ideas, and told me to send in a new expense account showing that I was staying overnight in a hotel and to cut down on the mileage. I did what they told me to do, and the final total on the new expense account was the same amount as that on the first one.

***

Once a month we had a staff meeting in Milwaukee on a Saturday. Normally, as I'd arrive I would step in each of the boss' offices and say hello, but on one particular morning I went straight to a desk and started to get my papers ready for the meeting.

The head boss came to the door of his office and said, "Gail. You didn't stop in to say hello."

I turned to face him and said, "Give me ten minutes of uninterrupted time and I'll prove to you that what I did was the best way to run my territory."

But he told me that he wouldn't give me the time, because he had checked it out like I had and said I was right in what I did. However, it didn't look good and he didn't want the Chicago office calling him to ask questions about how we were running the territory.

I wasn't very happy about it, and told him so, as I would be the guy on the end of the limb if anyone started an investigation, and checked with the hotels and/or motels and found my name wasn't listed on their records.

A couple of years later the company demanded receipts for hotel and/or motel stays, meals over

$25.00, as well as receipts for anything when a customer was involved. I was stationed at a different location when this happened, but I was glad to see it put in practice.

I couldn't then and I can't now figure out why some people were so worried of how other people were doing things and why they wanted everyone to fit a pattern. I always tried to do the best job I could under the circumstances, feeling that every place had its own quirks, and not the same prices as compared to other places.

*****

While I was working in Green Bay, my mother passed away. I was really upset with the doctor about Mother's death. She had cancer and was in real bad shape. The doctor was operating on her, and came down to tell us—Dad, Ardyth and I—that we had a choice. They could move organs around in her and she would live another six months, or they could sew her up and she would starve to death.

Dad looked at us and said, "She's your mother. What should we do?" He couldn't make the decision and wanted us to do it.

I said, "There is no way in hell Mother is going to starve to death." Ardyth agreed, so the doctor continued the operation and our mother lived in agony for close to six months before she died.

NEVER AGAIN. If the doctor would have told us an operation would keep her in pain for six more months and then she would die, or that he could close her up and medicate her so she doesn't feel the pain before she died quickly, I think we would have made a different choice. A choice that would have been a lot easier on her. In a situation like that it's better to end it quickly, as the person will die either way and they won't suffer as much. (This is what Neva and I want our children to do for us.)

***

Back in the late 1950s and early 1960s, there seemed to be a finance company on as many corners as bars were in downtown Green Bay, and due to sicknesses of the kids and myself, I think we borrowed from each one of them. There wasn't any health insurance to buy back then.

At one time, we had two kids in the hospital and then I had to join them to make it a threesome, and we had to borrow more money.

We managed to settle our debts with each one of the companies over a period of time, but it was tight for us for a long time.

Along with that, we learned sometimes, doctors don't use the right words explaining things. I had an operation on my big toes, and later lying in bed, Neva on one side the doctor on the other side, Neva said, "I'll have to do a lot of things for him as he won't be able to stand on his feet, won't I?"

The doctor replied, "No, he can take care of himself."

I'm lying in the bed listening, so when we get home and I'm there on the couch with my feet up, whenever I needed something I got up and did it.

Two days later my feet were swelling in the cast and hurting, so off to see the doctor I went.

In the exam room, the doctor told me I was on my feet too much. Getting angry, I told him I heard him tell Neva that she didn't have to help me. I could do things for myself, so what did he expect.

He broke the casts on my feet, put on two new ones and didn't say anything. He's retired now.

***

On several occasions, Neva's dad, my dad and Bob Haws would come up to visit us and we would go fishing in some of the small lakes that were deep in the woods. On one such fishing trip, my dad and Bob were in one boat and Neva's dad and I were in another when my father-in-law said, "I've got one."

I raised the motor, but the fish swam right under the boat and the line broke. We saw it and it looked like it was the size of a man. My father-in-law had tears in his eyes after losing that fish. I never saw a fish that big, but after seeing people spear sturgeon I now believe that was what the fish was.

Another time when Dad, Bob and I went fishing we went to a small lake.

Dad said, "That lake is too small to have any fish in it."

Bob commented, "Just sit and I'll make a few casts to see if I can raise anything."

On the second cast, Bob caught a four pound bass and the old man almost broke his leg trying to get out of the car fast enough. Dad was ecstatic. We caught more than enough fish to feed the families that day.

***

We were members of St. Paul's United Methodist Church in Green Bay for a while, and it was called the Railroad Church. As it was explained to me, the church first started near the railroad yards in Green Bay and later moved west to its present location. It still has some windows that have a railroad motif in them.

During the nine years we lived in Green Bay, we lived in three rented houses until we finally purchased a house. We had to move from the first house as the bathroom and bedrooms were upstairs, and Neva had developed a hiatus hernia and couldn't handle taking care of the children up and down the stairs, as she was pregnant with our third child. Janice arrived in November of 1956. It was time to move again, as we needed more room.

We moved to a one floor, two bedroom duplex. While we were there, the owner asked us to show the other half of the duplex to anyone who came by to see it. One day when I was home for lunch, there was a knock on our door. When I opened it, there stood Bart Starr and his wife. They wanted to look at the other side of the duplex. (If I remember correctly, Starr's wife wasn't interested in it, as it didn't have a mud room.)

Sometime after Janice was born, she started having problems that required her to be in constant care by doctors. They had x-rays done on her, and it showed she had four kidneys. Each regular kidney had another kidney attached to it, causing numerous infections to occur.

At that time, I asked her doctors if they could remove the extra kidneys and was advised they could not do that. If they removed anything, it would have to be a pair of them, which we were advised would not be a good idea, as she would then have only one set of kidneys. They didn't know which kidneys were infected. Finally, they were able to stop the infections with medication.

When Janice became an adult she checked the problem with her doctors and was advised that any one kidney could be removed and not affect the other kidneys. She was also advised that it is hereditary. (This is now her decision to make, and we hope everything turns out all right for her.)

***

Neva and I moved into a three-bedroom home on Roscoe Street. It had two bedrooms and a bath upstairs, and a bedroom and bathroom on the main level. We settled in after the first of the year of 1957. We stayed there for a while, and in February, 1959, we found out Neva was pregnant again. This time it was with our son, Douglas, who was born in November.

Now that we had one son, we agreed to try to have another son. Neva's doctor talked with her about it as he didn't want to see her get pregnant with another baby. He suggested that in the month of February, Neva should go to the east coast and I should go to the west coast, as the month of February was a bad month for us to be together, as the last two children were conceived in February.

Well, we proved he was right as our fourth daughter, Linda, was born in November, 1961. After her birth having ended up with four daughters and one son, we agreed that's it. No more children.

Late one night in 1962, Neva and I were sitting at the dinner table talking, the kids were in bed, and she was facing the window looking out at the driveway. With it being dark outside and the dining room light on inside, neither of us could see anything outside, only the reflection of ourselves in the window.

The next morning a neighbor lady across the street spoke with Neva. She asked her if she saw the man on our driveway jumping up and down with his pants down?

I'm not sure what Neva's reply was except that she hadn't. I wish I would have been there when our neighbor asked her. I would have asked, "Did you call the police, or did you watch the show?" Evidently the show was more important than getting the guy arrested, as she didn't call the police.

***

On one of our trips through the territory with my boss we were up in Iron Mountain for the night and went out for dinner. One thing led to another and by the time we were finished eating, we had had too much to drink. On the way back to the motel I told him I knew a short cut which required driving over the train tracks. For some reason, I was under the impression there was a walk-way between the rails, and since there wasn't, I hung up the car between the tracks.

We knew a passenger train was due in approximately an hour to an hour and a half, so we knew we had to do something quick to get the car out of the way.

I shifted gears, going backward and forward, and fortunately got the car off the tracks. However, I left the gas tank lying between the rails. I just kept going to the motel and walked back, and there was my boss standing, holding the gas tank.

The next morning we got the car fixed and were on our way to check out more of the territory. Got away with one of those nasty mistakes again. I honestly think I was very lucky. It could've been a lot worse.

***

During my time in Green Bay, the Milwaukee Railroad entered the field of Trailer-On-Flat-Car (TOFC) and Container-On-Flat-Car (COFC). My job was to make the surveys to see if the customers were interested in this type of service as well as what rates we could charge for it, and would it be profitable. The customers were certainly interested, and we built the service up where we were handling a lot of TOFC business.

At one of our Green Bay Traffic Club meetings in 1959, we arranged for the new coach of the Green Bay Packers to be our guest speaker. The president of the club was supposed to pick him up at his house, but when I arrived at the ballroom where we were holding the meeting, I was advised our president had broken his leg and couldn't drive. So I left to go pick him up. The coach gave a worthy speech and was well-received. His name was Vince Lombardi.

We also had annual dinners for the Traffic Club, where we had a party room to entertain customers and friends from other railroads. At one of the dinners, I was in the room in the morning setting it up to take care of our guests with drinks and appetizers when the phone rang so I answered it.

A voice said, "Mr. Meintzer, this is Agent Smith from the FBI. I know you're busy, but my partner and I have to talk with you about a problem."

I started laughing and said, "Okay, keep talking and I'll recognize your voice."

"No, we're not any of your railroad friends, but we are from the FBI."

I still didn't entirely believe the man, but said, "Okay, come on up."

In a few minutes there was a knock on the door, and when I opened it, there stood two complete strangers to me, each with an FBI badge in their hands. My stomach hit the floor. What could I say, but come in and what can I do for you?

The taller of the two agents said, "We don't want to take up too much of your time as we know this is a big day for you, but we do need some information."

I said okay, wondering what was going to happen.

The other agent said, "We understand you recently purchased a house, and we'd like to show you a list of names to see if you know any of the people listed."

He showed me the list and looking at it, I didn't see anyone I knew and said so. I also asked what this was all about, and he said, "All of the people listed here used the same realtor, and there are problems with the paper work, and government agencies are involved."

"I used my G.I. privilege from World War II to get a G.I. loan. What trouble are we in?"

They advised me that we weren't in trouble, we were the victims and we were paying more than we should've been.

In 1964, the company transferred me to Milwaukee and promoted me to the title of Sales Representative, Rail Highways Sales for the state of Wisconsin so we sold the house and went to renting.

While it was a good job, it also had a big drawback. It's difficult to work a job when you have two bosses with different ideas. The traffic manager in Milwaukee was in charge of all freight sales in Wisconsin, and the boss in Chicago was in charge of all rail-highway sales nationwide, so I was getting conflicted orders of what to do from each of them.

Finally, I went to my boss in Milwaukee, who I had worked for before and told him it wasn't working out too well.

He told me he would look into it, and it wasn't very long that I was promoted to Assistant General Agent in Milwaukee. I no longer reported to the general agent, instead I reported to the traffic manager. I was getting used to seeing the comment, "Check into this" whenever he didn't want to do something. He turned it over to me to handle, saying, "Tell me how it turns out."

Occasionally, the general agent or the assistant traffic manager would call me into their office and ask me what was going on.

I simply said, "Your salesmen are not doing their job, and the boss is sending me out to get it corrected. Don't look or blame me, step on your salesmen to get them straightened out."

***

While we were living in Milwaukee one winter, we went to one of the county golf courses, as they allowed people to toboggan there. I picked a spot that looked good, put the kids on the toboggan with me on the tail end, and off we went.

Before I realized what was happening, we were headed to go over a sand trap where the top of it was a good three or four feet higher than the bottom of the trap. When we landed, I got such a jolt I was seeing stars.

We eventually came to a stop and started back up the hill, me hurting really bad. I said we were going to move over to another spot that appeared to be such that we would not go over the sand trap. BIG MISTAKE AGAIN. We got on the toboggan, and I'll be damned if it didn't go over the same sand trap. My butt got a real wallop, so bad it ended the tobogganing for the day.

The next day I was at the doctor's office being seen for the injury. Wouldn't you know it, x-rays showed I had damaged my back. The doctor told me not to pick up anything heavy, and to stay off the toboggan.

***

In June of 1966, the general agent in Chicago retired. I attended his retirement party in Chicago and the vice president of the sales department stopped by my table and talked with me for a while. He appeared to be very happy to see me there. A few days later, I was appointed as General Agent in Chicago.

The order of the Chicago office was this: a traffic manager was in charge over all of it. An assistant traffic manager was in charge of the traveling sales agents outside of Chicago. My position of General Agent made me in charge of eleven salesmen in

Chicago, four clerks, two secretaries, plus I had fifteen large national accounts to handle. Accounts such as Armour & Co., Swift & Co., Wilson & Co., International Harvester, U. S. Gypsum, Allied Mills, Edward Hines Lumber Co., Bemis Bag Co., and U. S. Steel. (It was so long ago I can't remember the rest of them.)

Shortly after I started in Chicago, the company decided to have a three-week sales effort to show off our new train service between Chicago and Seattle, Washington. It meant spending 24 hours a day at work, calling on customers and being in a hotel for meetings, as well as entertaining customers for lunch and dinner.

After it was over and I was finally able to go back to Milwaukee to be with my family, Neva asked me what I wanted for dinner. I replied, "Tomato soup and a grilled cheese sandwich." I was tired of all the rich food I had been eating and drinking during the sales effort.

Later that night after I fell asleep, Neva, in rolling over, touched me.

I jumped out of bed, yelling, "What are you doing in my bed? I'm a married man."

The next day we both had a big laugh about it, but it did startle me as I wasn't used to sleeping with someone.

Shortly thereafter, we moved back to Deerfield. Mother had passed away and I was head of our

Chicago Sales forces, so Dad was now living with us. When I was a kid, my father had worked at the brickyard on County Line Road, which is now known as Lake-Cook road, would occasionally see limousines stop on the side of the road and transfer something from one to the other, and always wondered what was going on. He would tell me about it every evening when we were home.

The bar owner of Dirty Helen's wrote a book and it was published, but it was after my father died in January, 1967. It's too bad my dad never got to read her book, as it would have solved his inquiry about the two limousines that used to exchange something frequently by the brickyard in the 1930s. It was bootleg liquor, as liquor was outlawed during prohibition.

***

As General Agent, I became a member of the Chicago Traffic Club, who had their headquarters on the second floor of the Palmer House Hotel in Chicago. Every Friday if I wasn't tied up, I would go there for lunch as their Filet of Sole was out-of-this-world and I had the opportunity to talk with customers, as well as have friendly connections—being other railroads that we had good relations with and could concur with on establishing through freight rates when we needed to.

We had an occasional problem in the office. One day I noticed a clerk was missing. I called the chief clerk and asked him where this certain clerk was. He told me he called in sick. For some reason, something registered in my mind that something was wrong, so I told him to bring in his book on attendance.

"How many days has he been off sick, and what days of the week were they?" I asked when he came into my office. The chief check showed the man's sick days were only on Mondays and Fridays.

I told the chief clerk to bring him in my office as soon as the man came in tomorrow, along with his attendance book.

The next day, they were in my office bright and early, and I told the clerk I wanted to know how he only gets sick on Mondays and Fridays. The man admitted then that he wasn't actually sick. He would be invited to a weekend party and he needed Friday off to travel there and sometimes after the party he wasn't "feeling too well" so he'd call in sick on Monday.

That didn't bode well with me, so I told him he better look for another job because he wasn't going to be working in my office very long. It wasn't too long after that he bid in a job in the yard office, and we were rid of him. (Trust, respect and integrity are more important than partying every weekend in my book.)

***

During my time in Chicago, there were two secretaries working in the office, one who worked for me exclusively, and the other who worked for both the traffic manager and the assistant traffic manager, though both secretaries reported to me. I was reading some correspondence in my office when the assistant traffic manager walked in, closed the door, sat down, looked at me and said, "Gail, I've got a problem and need your help."

I looked at him and said, "What's the problem?"

"I'm afraid of our secretary, and I'm wondering if you would exchange secretaries with me?"

I couldn't stop from laughing, as it was difficult for me to picture that man being afraid of a secretary. "Is this a joke or for real?"

He replied, "I mean it. I'm uncomfortable having her in my office."

"Well, I've never used her before, but if it helps you out I'll make the switch right now."

He went back to his office, and I called both ladies into my office separately. I explained what was going to happen immediately, explaining to my secretary that the switch had nothing to do with her work. Unless I was out calling on a large account customer or with one of my salesmen, I would be dictating letters to the other secretary on files that needed my attention.

One day I had to dictate a letter regarding the proposed sale of some railroad property we owned in Chicago to a customer, I needed to explain how it would affect the sales department business. This kind of correspondence was very complicated and took a lot of time, as we had to look back into old files that went back in some cases 100 years or more. I had already researched the file, putting flags in for certain pages I wanted to refer to, so I called in my new secretary and told her this correspondence was going to take time. If she had to excuse herself, she should say so and I'd continue after she returned.

After about an hour she said, "Mr. Meintzer, you have to go faster. I *also* have other things to do."

Now I knew what the assistant traffic manager was referring to when he had come in to see me about her. I stopped, sat back in my chair, looked at her and said, "Evidently, you don't know that I'm the boss in this office, and when I'm dictating to you *that* is the only thing you have to be concerned about."

In less than a week, she found a job elsewhere and put in her resignation notice.

The next time I saw the assistant traffic manager in his office, I walked in and said, "Find yourself a secretary, I'm taking mine back."

Concerned, he looked at me and asked, "What happened?"

I shrugged. "She decided to quit."

"What did you do to get her to quit?"

"She thought she could run this office and I convinced her who the boss was here. She realized it was in her best interests to move on."

Chicago was a great place to work, something was going on all the time.

***

I enjoyed the activities at the Chicago Traffic Club. They had a dinner dance almost every month. At these dinner dances, we would have a number of liquor bottles open at the end of the festivities that couldn't be turned back in, so we had to get rid of them. The best way to do that was to take them home with us. Very seldom did I have to go to a liquor store.

At one of the dinners, Neva and I caused quite a scene and had the attention of most of those present. Neva had bridgework done in her mouth, and while the food was being served her bridgework moved as a server accidently bumped her in the back. It stuck into her tongue and the bleeding started.

I was talking with some other people when it happened and didn't notice her make a motion to another lady friend to come with her to the ladies room. They couldn't stop the bleeding, and her friend came back to tell me I was needed in the ladies room as Neva was bleeding in her mouth.

I asked her to see if a doctor was available in the ballroom and I headed for the ladies room. I stopped at the door, as I didn't want to cause any more trouble and asked someone to bring her out. Her friend pushed me on my back through the door, saying "You're going in, Neva's bleeding."

Someone got a doctor, and he took a look before he told me to get her to a hospital. There wasn't anything he could do here.

We grabbed a cab and I told him to get us to the nearest hospital emergency room. The medical staff eventually got the bleeding stopped, so we headed back to the Palmer House where we had a room for the night. We weren't concerned about the dinner dance anymore, as it was very late in the evening and I wanted Neva to get rest. She had quite an exciting night.

I enjoyed bowling in the Traffic Club Bowling League, but there were also a number of members who enjoyed playing gin rummy. Every year, they had a gin rummy tournament, and one year, I was lucky to win the championship trophy. I have no idea of where it is now, probably lost in one of our many moves. I also had a lot of bowling trophies, but Neva got tired of their sitting around collecting dust, so they ended up in the garage where they finally disappeared.

***

I was still in the Chicago sales office when the company had some problems in our Los Angeles sales office. The district sales manager got in some trouble, and the company transferred him to the Davenport, Iowa office.

The assistant traffic manager in our office had been transferred to San Francisco for the traffic manager job covering all of California, so I called the traffic manager in San Francisco and asked what happened. He told me what happened, along with what the company was paying him, which really surprised me as it was much more than I was getting paid. He also had a lot less responsibility.

I told him he owed me a favor, as I had taken care of getting rid of the secretary he couldn't handle. I asked him to call the vice president and ask him to transfer me out to California.

The man said he'd love to have me out there with him, and did call the vice president asking for the transfer, but the vice president told him there was no way that would happen, as I was doing too good a job in Chicago.

The traffic manager called me back and told me what happened, so I called the vice president's office. The vice president's assistant answered, and I told him I would like to have an appointment with the vice president. The assistant set it up for the next day.

As I came into the office for the meeting with the

vice president, he said, "Gail, there is no way I'll send you to a small office like Los Angeles.

I said, "I'm happy with my job and my wages, but there is a problem. The general agents in Los Angeles, St. Louis, Denver, Sioux City, Dubuque and Sioux Falls all have higher salaries than I do, so they should be in charge of bigger agencies. I'll be happy to go to any one of those agencies with my salary."

A couple of weeks later, I received a nice raise in salary that took me above the other agencies. (It's important to do comprehensive research.)

***

Another thing we lived through that was very difficult was the death of Neva's father shortly after he and Neva's mother came back from a trip to Florida. He was having trouble on the way home with his driving, as he had difficulty seeing. The reason for the difficulty turned out to be an aneurysm in his head, and while we were there in the hospital, he passed away. I liked to be in his company and he was a great father-in-law. I especially enjoyed talking with him about the railroad.

It was a neat relationship we had. Even though he was a union employee and I was in management, we could still talk about the problems on the railroad without arguing. I'll never forget him.

Our daughter, Pam, and her husband, Jim, who passed away previously, had two bricks personalized—one for Neva and I, and one for Grandpa Jewell. The bricks now rest together on the west side of the railroad station at the National Railroad Museum in Green Bay, Wisconsin.

Meintzer and Haws kids, early 1960s

Gail Meintzer and Ardyth Haws, June 1969

Neva, Pam, and Gail Meintzer on April 12, 1972
on Pam's wedding day

Neva and Gail Meintzer, late 1980s

Chapter 7

When I left Green Bay for Milwaukee, I had to give up the company season tickets for the Green Bay Packers' football games. Consequently, I applied for four season tickets. In the fall of 1969, I was notified by the Packers' association that I would receive four season tickets starting with the 1970-1971 season. Unfortunately, I wasn't able to use them. I had to find someone to buy them from me for the year.

The first year, I sold them to a friend on the GB & W Railroad in Chicago. After the season was over, he advised he didn't want them the next season, so I started looking for a buyer. I sold the tickets this time to our local agent in Green Bay, and he took them for the next seventeen years, as I was away from the area that long.

160

We didn't know it would be seventeen years at the time, as we did not know there would be more transfers to other areas. As it turned out, we remained in Seattle for twenty-two months.

When the Great Northern, Northern Pacific and the Chicago, Burlington & Quincy Railroad merged into the Burlington Northern Railroad, our company, Milwaukee Road wanted to "beef up" our sales force on the west coast, so they transferred several of us out there. I was promoted to Assistant Traffic Manager, Sales in Seattle, Washington. I was in Seattle for several months alone, as Neva and I had difficulty selling our house in Deerfield, Illinois.

The company took care of our expenses for the first month and then we were on our own, so I found a cheap hotel I could pay for by the week. I didn't know it at the time, but there were a number of prostitutes working out of that hotel. After a while it came to my attention, and I asked a few questions about it. I was advised that yes, they did, but they would not bother or approach anyone staying at the hotel.

The hotel was in the downtown area close to restaurants and movie theaters. One of the fellows would drop me off on his way home and pick me up in the morning. After I got to the hotel, I would change clothes, go out to eat, take in a movie, go back to the hotel and stop in the coffee shop to have coffee until 9:50 p.m., when I would tell the waitress I had to go to my room for my phone call.

Before I was transferred out to Seattle, the manager of communications for the company told me that he had set up an arrangement, whereby my wife could call into the company phone operators, identify herself, and they would put her through on the company's Watts line. It allowed for Neva and I to talk each night without paying for long distance phone calls (which could get very expensive in those days). There were some rules: 1st-talk important family business, 2nd -talk family business, 3rd -talk anything. That way, if the operator cut in to hang up, we had said what we needed to say. It also meant the line was needed for company business. It worked great and cost us minimum telephone charges from Deerfield to Seattle.

The waitress in the coffee shop at night also worked at the Golden Tides restaurant, north of Seattle. As we spent time talking while I was having coffee, we got to know each other. When I told her that my wife finally sold the house and was coming out with the kids, she told me to be sure to come out to the restaurant for a Crab Louie Salad. She said to tell the waitress who I was, as she was the pantry chef that made them. "You'll really get a good one, then."

After the kids and Neva came to Seattle and we were settled in, I called her one day and told Neva that I was picking her up to go to lunch in 20 minutes. We went to the Golden Tides restaurant and got a booth for two. I told the waitress we wanted two Crab Louie Salads, and to tell the pantry chef we were here. She brought out two salads, the likes I've never seen before or since, and we started to eat. Two fellows came in, sat in a booth across the aisle from us, and looked at the salads we were eating.

When the waitress came by and asked for their order, they both said they'd like a Crab Louis Salad. When their order was placed on the table, they looked at theirs, turned and looked at ours and shook their heads. The salads sure didn't look anywhere near the same. It was a case of who you knew.

***

Over the years working for the Milwaukee Road, I had always heard comments about being in Seattle was like working in paradise. I found a four-bedroom home overlooking everyone's back yard from its place on top of the hill of Puget Sound for us to rent. The owner told me as we were new to the area, that he would have a gardener come in to take care of the flowers and shrubbery. I only had to mow the lawn, and it cost $250.00 per month.

The first three weeks we were there, it did look

like paradise with the sun shining and the mountains in the background. The rest of the year was much different—overcast and raining. Rain out there is not the same as rain in the Midwest. It's more like a mist most of the time and overcast.

It was during that time, I noticed that all of our five kids who had blonde hair didn't any longer. One evening when I came home, Neva was in the kitchen making supper as a couple of the girls came walking into the living room. I noticed their hair was dark and said, "Neva, why aren't the kids washing their hair?"

The voice from the kitchen said, "If the sun ever comes out, their hair will be blonde again."

One thing we did that we didn't do elsewhere was go on "day" trips on weekends to see the countryside. It was a good thing we did, as we weren't out there very long.

Just before I was transferred out there, the Boeing Company, which was the largest employer out there at the time had lost a large contract and laid off close to 60,000 people. It started a ripple effect, and other companies laid off people as their businesses were hit also. The area was really depressed. There were bill boards along the sides of the main highways that read, *The last person leaving should turn off the lights,* in reference to people leaving due to the loss of jobs.

We had to purchase a new sofa. We went to Sears,

located nearby in a six-story high building and asked which floor had furniture. We were told it was on the fifth floor, so we went up there to take a look around and see what they had.

At first we couldn't find a salesman, but then finally found one laying on a sofa resting who apparently thought he didn't have any customers coming in. We shocked him by asking to purchase a sofa. That was how bad the lay-offs effected the markets.

***

When I had some free time on a weekend, I went down to the local bowling alley to bowl a few lines. As I turned my bowling sheet in that showed my scores, the counterman mentioned my scores were really good and asked if I was interested in league bowling. I told him my job required a lot of traveling, and that it would depend on what night the league bowled.

The bowling alley was looking for a good bowler to be on their house team on Wednesday and Thursday nights. I told him Wednesday night was out of the question, but Thursday night was doable.

The team was good and we participated in the play-off for the championship. Just before we began bowling, our captain, the opposing team's captain, and the secretary/treasurer were off to the side talking rather urgently. When our captain came back, nothing was said, and we started bowling.

Our team won the championship and the secretary/treasurer paid our team off. Afterward, we went to a Chinese joint for drinks and something to eat. Our captain gave each of us $200.00 since the team had received $1000.00 for winning the championship. One of the fellows asked what the meeting had been about and the captain told us, "The secretary/treasurer had a financial problem and used some of the league money to take care of it. They didn't have enough to pay everyone off that had money coming to them."

After hearing what happened, I commented he made the right choice paying us off or I would have called the police to accuse him for stealing. They didn't know what to say in response.

I went to tell them I ran into a similar problem in high school when a team in the league didn't show up a lot of times. They were short on the prize money and we didn't get the proper pay-off. It wasn't going to happen a second time to me.

I started bowling again the next season with the team, but had to quit in late January due to being transferred again, this time to Des Moines, Iowa.

***

After living in Seattle for a while, I realized that

our 25th (Silver) wedding anniversary was not too far away. I began stashing away silver dollars. If I remember correctly, a total of 237 of them, the price of an airline round trip ticket from Seattle to Chicago, and return so that Neva could use it any time she wanted to or needed to go home to see her mother.

By the time June 21, 1972 came around, we were living in Des Moines, Iowa. We planned on having the dinner party at The Milk Pail Restaurant in Elgin, as it was closest to most of the relatives. We stayed at Chy & Jim's house,(Neva's sister and brother-in-law's) and just before we left for the party, I gave the silver dollars to the kids and told them to make a large heart with an arrow going through it and to write underneath the words, "I love you."

When we came home Neva would see it first. She did, and she loved it. She returned one of the silver dollars to me as a keepsake, and I still carry it around in my pocket, dated 1972.

***

Over the summer, our son, Douglas, needed a job, so I contacted one of our operating officials. Doug got a job as a "gandy dancer" on a section crew in the Mason City, Iowa area. The pay was good and he found out what hard work was—real hard work.

It was a different story with my job in Des Moines.

That was a sticky situation being transferred to Des Moines, as the Federal government had some rules that we would get in trouble for if the company transferred me with a promotion and raise, as I was already making more money than the person I was replacing. My new position as Assistant Regional Manager, Sales was at the same pay. Two months later, the company promoted me to Regional Manager, Sales and gave me a raise. The sales territory covered areas of Iowa, South Dakota, and Nebraska. This position also put me on the Board of Directors of the Des Moines Union Railroad, of which the company was half owners along with the Norfolk and Western Railroad.

Our sales offices in Des Moines, Davenport, Cedar Rapids, Mason City, Sioux City, Sioux Falls, and Omaha all reported to me. I arrived in Des Moines just as the big Grain Sale to Russia began. I was hearing people referring to "beans," and had no idea what beans they were referring to. I knew about green beans, kidney beans, lima beans, navy beans, and wax beans, but I couldn't picture shipping those kinds of beans in railroad covered hopper cars. Then I heard someone make a comment about "soybeans" and everything fell into place for me.

Elevator operators along our railroad wanted to put in or extend their sidetracks so they had enough room to load 25, 50 and 75 car grain trains. I spent quite a lot of time working with these elevator operators, the Iowa Department of Transportation, and our other departments on extending side tracks so they could load these grain trains to take advantage of the lower freight rates by loading longer trains. The grain trains went from Iowa stations to Mississippi, and to Louisiana ocean ports in Baton Rouge and New Orleans areas for shipment to Russia.

As it took so long to have a train do a round trip, we worked out an arrangement with one grain buyer in Davenport, whereby he purchased a lot of grain from a group of small elevator operators between Perry and Cedar Rapids where we could run a 25-car grain train on a daily basis, and the operators could load two to six cars in a short time.

We would set out the right amount of cars each would need on their side tracks for that day's loading, and we would start a train from Perry to pick up the loaded cars, take them to Davenport—where they would be dumped into barges—and the train would start back towards Perry, setting off cars ordered by the elevator operators at night so they would be ready to load first thing in the morning. It worked out beautiful, and we had maximum utilization from the equipment. It was actually a better money maker for us than the large grain trains due to the car utilization.

An elevator operator west of Mason City called

and complained about a larger elevator loading grain trains not according to the rules governing the freight rates. This was something I needed to look into personally, so on a trip I made to Chicago for a meeting, I arranged another meeting with our engineering department to check the track plans for this particular elevator.

I had a copy of the plans made to take back to my office in Des Moines. (This is where my taking a class in blue print reading in high school paid off.) Checking the size of the cars and trackage involved showed that while there was enough trackage to handle a 75-car grain train, the trackage wasn't configured properly. Only 69 cars could be loaded and then the switch on one end was fouled. The only thing that could be done was for their engine to come out on railroad trackage to move the cars—which was illegal, or for our engine to move the cars for them to load more, which was also illegal.

I checked where one of their grain trains was at when it was coming back from the Gulf Coast, and saw it would be set on their trackage for loading on a Monday. That Sunday night I traveled to Mason City and called my district manager there and requested that he have breakfast with me on Monday morning.

He asked if there was a problem, and I told him we'd talk about it in the morning. After breakfast, we went down to the railroad. I had told him that he was to sit in his car at one switch point and I'd sit in my car at the other switch point, and we would watch the operators load their grain train. They couldn't help but see our cars, and knew something was up.

Finally, the trainmaster from Mason City came out and asked what was going on. I told him that we wanted to watch the loading of their grain train.

He said, "You're making them awfully nervous sitting here."

I replied, "They should be nervous; they know they can't load a 75-car train without violating the rules, and they're going to stop doing it. The other elevator operators are complaining and I don't blame them for it."

I found out not much later as I returned to my office in Des Moines that the elevator operator had called their Des Moines office, who in turn called their New York City office, who called our vice president in Chicago. The vice president tried to call me, but as cell phones didn't exist yet, they had no way of reaching me.

I returned the call to the vice president, and when he asked what was going on, I told him the truth. That what was happening near Mason City violated the freight rate rules, and I had stopped it. Either they had to fix the configuration of their trackage by moving a switch several hundred feet, or they had to load 50-car trains instead and pay the rate that corresponded, which of course was higher.

There weren't any more questions about the situation.

***

From the time I was stationed in Green Bay as a Traveling Freight Agent back in 1955 through 1964 I used to join a group of fellows in the transportation industry that went "up north" to have a weekend of fun, drinking, playing cards, golfing, fishing, and lots of conversation. Even when I went back to Milwaukee and Chicago, I would still get together with them twice a year, in spring and fall. The transfer to Seattle made it difficult, due to the distance involved, but when I was in Des Moines, the distance wasn't too bad, so we were able to get together again.

One of the fellows and I got interested in a topic of conversation, so we had a bottle of scotch and sat down to discuss it. Not paying attention to the time or amount we were drinking while we talked, we finally realized the scotch was gone, stopped talking, and hit the beds to go to sleep.

When I woke up the next morning, I realized I couldn't move my right arm. I mentioned it to the group, and one of the fellows said, "You might have had a stroke."

One fellow drove me to the local hospital and I

had them examine me to see what was wrong. After the examination was finished, the doctor said they couldn't find anything wrong and cleared me to go. I went back to the cottage we were using, and as the weekend was coming to an end, I headed to Des Moines and home.

After being home for a few days and still not feeling any better, Neva and I decided it would be a good idea to see another doctor, which I did, and ended up being admitted into the hospital.

About two days later, a doctor walked in and said, "Your doctor suggested I talk with you."

I said okay, so he asked me a number of questions about what had happened the day before I woke up. I told him how we fished while others played golf during the day, then we had cocktails and dinner, and then played poker in the evening with some sitting around, talking.

"You and the other gentleman sat and talked, drinking scotch on the rocks, while doing so for several hours.

I said, "That's right."

He looked at me and asked, "Have you ever heard of 'Saturday Night Palsy?'"

"No," I said, "what's that?"

"When you go to sleep and have your arm in a position that cuts off the blood flow and the pain that you feel makes you roll over or move your arm to a different position, and you continue to sleep.

But when you drink too much like you did, then it dulls your senses. You don't feel the pain, and your arm becomes paralyzed. It should be alright by the end of the month."

And it was. I made a point to be sure I never drank that much again.

***

Our daughter, Marcia, had enlisted in the U.S. Army and attended training at a camp in the south. During her training, she had health problems. As the U.S. Army couldn't place her in the position she requested when she enlisted, she received an honorable discharge and returned to Des Moines where she had a follow up appointment for her health issues.

Neva and I received a call from Marcia when she was nineteen-years-old letting us know that she was in the hospital, and asking if one of us could be there with her, as the doctors were going to tell her what was wrong and she was very concerned.

I told her I would be there as quickly as I could as I wanted to hear what the doctors would say. We hadn't known there was anything wrong with her.

I was sitting there, waiting with her when the doctors walked in. They told Marcia that the Mayo Clinic and Baylor University had both reported back on the specimens they received from the hospital, and both indicated that she had Lupus Erythematosus, an autoimmune disease. They went on to say they anticipated her life span would only be another twenty years. I was stunned.

I didn't really know what the hell to say, it was such a shock to me. She sounded happy and relieved, as she thought she was dying *now*. I finally recovered enough to say that no one can be sure of how long they would live, and there can be any type of accident that will cut a person's life short. (I'm happy that she listened to the doctors, followed their advice, and celebrated her sixty-first birthday in August, 2016, out-living what the doctors thought would happen.)

***

Several years later, the company made a major change in our department and I was appointed Area Manager, Sales. The agencies in Oklahoma, Missouri, and Texas, specifically in Tulsa, Kansas City, Houston and Dallas were added to my territory. I had my hands full, and thank God, I had a good secretary. There were times when I would be gone for a week at a time and I told all of the district managers that when she *called* for information, it would be the same as if I called them, and I didn't want to hear any complaints.

Many times I would leave home on Sunday

afternoon for Texas and on Friday, before boarding a plane, I would call my secretary to ask what I had to face when I returned.

She would reply, "I have the mail sorted in piles from 'see now' to 'Circular file' and some stuff we have to handle on Saturday. I'll see you at 9:30 in the morning. We should be finished by noon."

I would ask her to call Neva and tell her to feed the kids, and meet me at the airport. We'd have dinner on the way home, which Neva always enjoyed. (I always drove my car when I was working with the Iowa, Nebraska, and South Dakota Agencies.)

My secretary was one of the leading forces in starting the Des Moines Women's Traffic Club. I managed to get her an expense account from the company. She was doing such a good job running their Traffic Club that I received a call from an old friend who was on a committee of Traffic Clubs International. He asked if I would approve their putting her on the ballot to run for the position of Director, Rail.

I replied, "Old friend, do you just want a name, or in your own mind, does she have a chance of winning?"

He replied, "Gail, she has a 50-50 chance of winning."

I said, "Okay, put her name on the ballot." Dammed, if she didn't win the election. Now my job was to get Chicago to increase her expense account for the added traveling she would do.

***

One thing I really enjoyed in Des Moines, which I've never seen elsewhere, are restaurants in large grocery stores. While you're shopping, or after you're done shopping, you can go in the restaurant and order your breakfast, lunch or dinner, pay and be on your way.

Periodically, we would see a man come in with his wife, who, from the looks of it, evidently had a serious stroke.

To me, the way that man took care of his wife was amazing, and I would think to myself that I hoped I could be the man he was if such a thing came into our life.

Today, I'm faced with something similar. Not as bad as that woman was, but something that has changed our lives. While Neva was in the hospital with pneumonia, she was talking to the doctor and had two T.I.A.s (like a mini stroke). The CT scan didn't show anything, but an MRI showed she had between eighty to one hundred of them in the past. Her brain had been seriously damaged, and it had become difficult for her to do things on her own and know what's happening around her. (I have a woman come in to clean on a regular basis, as well as another woman to do the laundry and help Neva bathe.)

I love my wife very much and do my best to give her all she desires. The one thing that baffles me the most is our meals. I would prefer to eat one major meal (lunch or dinner) at a restaurant, and breakfast and one lite meal at home, as Neva can't cook anymore since she can't stand long enough to do so. It puts me in the position of Chief Cook and Bottle Washer, and I don't know how to cook.

One of our daughters, Janice, wrote up some recipes for me, and when I tried to teach myself how to cook, I couldn't handle it. I went to frozen entrees, thinking I could heat them up, serve them, eat them, and problem taken care of.

It worked for a while—until I noticed I was getting very large ankles, legs and feet. Too much sodium, I was told with another trip to the doctor. I was eating too much salt, and told to change my medication, and check labels very closely. I not only have to watch the sodium, I also have to watch the fat as well as the cholesterol. If I had known then as I do now, I don't think I would have eaten so high on the hog as I did, with butter on my steak, a pat of butter each time I took a bite of a roll, butter and sour cream on each baked potato. My list could go on and on. Like one boss told me, "Gail, you have a champagne appetite on a beer expense account."

Thank God, I have four excellent doctors that have kept me alive so far, but boy, it was good back then. I even put some weight on. I'm working on how to serve the right food for both of us, hoping that someday I'll get it right.

***

In all forty years that I worked for the Milwaukee Road, I never lost control with a customer—until one day in Des Moines. I received a phone call from a small elevator owner in Northern Iowa complaining about our grain trains using all the covered hopper cars, and that he was going to need one car in May. This was in February, and that's when I lost it.

I told him that I had just finished calls from the Interstate Commerce Commission, the United States Department of Agriculture, and the Iowa Department of Transportation because customers were complaining about the big car shortage, and other customers were complaining because there were cars coming to them in a train that was stuck in the snow between Chicago and Savanna, Illinois, and I wasn't going to take any complaints from him or anyone else about something that was going to happen in May, and hung up the phone.

Then, realizing what I did, I called the assistant to the vice president and told him what happened and to expect a phone call from that particular customer. He advised he would take care of it and hung up.

The customer never called the Chicago office, but he must have done some checking, as he called me about three weeks later and apologized for yelling at me.

***

Things changed drastically for many railroad companies when the 1970s hit. The Rock Island Railroad entered into bankruptcy in 1975, and Milwaukee Road entered into bankruptcy in 1977. The creditors of the Rock Island Line advocated for the shutdown and liquidation of the property. The Milwaukee Road was a transcontinental railroad, so they looked to see if they could find a way to slim the trackage down as it was difficult to maintain all of the trackage we had. They agreed to get rid of the lines from Seattle east to the twin cities in Minnesota, a lot of the branch lines in Iowa were sold to other railroads or eliminated, and so in 1980 my job in Des Moines was also eliminated, along with all other positions in the office.

The company transferred the man that had a similar job to mine in Minneapolis to another department, and I became Area Manager, Sales in Minneapolis. I was responsible for the area of Minnesota, North Dakota, South Dakota, and the eastern half of Montana, including the provinces of Manitoba and Saskatchewan in Canada.

We rented a house in the northern area of Minneapolis. After several months, I had to go to Chicago for a meeting, so I thought I would drive down and take Neva with me so she could visit her mother and sister. Our five children were all out of the nest now, and living on their own. While we were down in Chicago someone had broken into our house and burglarized it, but we didn't find out until we got back. Thank God, I had asked Neva to come with me, as I certainly wouldn't have wanted her to be alone when someone broke into the house. I can't even imagine living one day without her in my life.

Gail Meintzer, golfing, 2007

Gail and Neva Meintzer at Mitch and Rebecca's
wedding, April 4, 2009

Gail Meintzer with character, Maxine,
at a flea market in 2009

Chapter 8

I made several trips to Winnipeg, Manitoba to meet with the Canadian National Railroad representatives on fertilizer business that originated in Saskatchewan, Canada. But in March of 1982, they abolished my job in Minneapolis, created a new position in Chicago, and transferred me there to become Director, Intermodal Sales.

I worked exclusively with shippers agents, or as we called them, third parties. They secured the business from the shippers, contracted with us to handle the trailer-loads or container-loads from the point of origin to destinations on our own railroad or destinations on other railroads, and move it in conjunction with those railroads. They would deal with cartage companies to deliver the trailers to us, and from the destination carrier to the consignee. I was responsible for this service for the United

States and Canada. During the time I had this job I made a large number of trips to both Winnipeg and Mississauga, a suburb of Toronto, Ontario.

By this time, there were several railroads that were interested in purchasing the Milwaukee Road out of bankruptcy court—The Grand Trunk Western, owned by the Canadian National Railroad; The Chicago and Northwestern Railroad and the Soo Line Railroad, who's biggest stockholder was the Canadian Pacific Railroad. The bankruptcy judge chose the Soo Lines offer in February, 1985, and we continued to operate as we did before.

We would get calls from salesmen on the Soo Line asking us to establish intermodal rates between two points on the Soo Line, and we told them we couldn't do it. We could only establish intermodal rates on our own lines, or in connection with some other railroad.

Their response was, "You fellows do it faster than our fellows, and by the time they get it done, the business is gone." I knew what they were referring to, as we used to have that condition for the Milwaukee Road.

***

I received a notice one day that the National Association of Shippers Agents was going to hold their annual convention in Vancouver, B.C. After I read it, I called in my reservations for my wife and myself, reserved our hotel room and got our airline reservations.

The assistant vice president of the Milwaukee Road I reported to came in and asked if I knew about the convention. He wanted me to be sure to attend, and I told him I had already put my reservation in.

He looked at me and said, "Good, I don't know why I worry about you, Gail. You always have everything covered."

My counterpart on the Soo Line called about it as well, asking if I was going to go. I replied, "Yes, I have all of my reservations made for my wife and I."

He asked, "How do you get approval from your vice president and president so fast?"

"What are you talking about?" I said.

He replied that they had to put in a request through their vice president's office and it needed to be approved by their president.

I laughed, saying when we're in a job like ours, we have the authority to run the department we're responsible for. He couldn't believe it.

Working in this job, Neva and I went to conventions in Long Boat Key, Florida; Boston, Massachusetts; and in San Diego and Palm Springs, California. Neva went to all of them with me on the expense account. Yes, this job had some good "perks" to it.

***

In June of 1985, the Soo Line gave a large number of us a proposal to take an early retirement offer. For me, it was a year's salary over two years, health insurance until Neva and I were both sixty-five years old, and a life insurance policy. There were several ways to consider it, and I took the one that should I die, Neva would receive my full benefits until she passed away.

There was a catch involved that read something like if necessary, they could hold us for a period of three months. I still don't know exactly why they held onto me, but now I'm glad they did. I found out much later when I applied for our railroad retirement. There was a rule that should your wife outlive you, she will receive your total railroad retirement, provided you retire within six months of your sixtieth birthday, or after.

If it is more than six months, she will receive your Social Security portion, but not the additional railroad retirement portion.

Knowing we were going to retire in the month of September, 1985, we decided we would move back to Green Bay, Wisconsin, as we had many friends there, we liked the area, and it was within driving distance of four of our five kids, and it wasn't wall-to-wall people like Chicago was. The pace of living was sedate.

We bought a home and started to relax, I played golf, we went to restaurants to eat, visited with friends, and enjoyed life.

I had sold our Packer season tickets in April, so I didn't have them while we were living in Green Bay now, but I did tell the fellow I sold them to that I wouldn't be selling them anymore.

Then, I received a phone call from a good friend I used to work with on the Milwaukee Road. He asked if he could take Neva and I out to dinner, as he was going to be in town in a few days and wanted to discuss something with me. Naturally I said, "Yes, we'd be happy to go."

We went out to a nice restaurant and during dinner he said he would like to pick my brain about intermodal business on the railroad.

I told him I thought we made a big mistake on the Milwaukee Road, trying to be all things for everyone, and in some cases, we were competing against ourselves. I continued to say, "I would recommend that the railroad should operate only on what is called Plan Two and a Half, Ramp to Ramp. That's where the railroad has complete control on what they do best.

He mentioned the group he was with was going to buy some of the trackage from the Soo Line that they didn't use after they bought the Milwaukee Road. In October, 1987, they were planning to start operations with this new railroad.

A few days later, I received a call from him again, this time asking me if I would act as a consultant for them in the Wisconsin area. (This could have been a very sticky situation for me, as you can't work for a railroad when you're drawing railroad retirement at the same time.)

I checked with some companies I used to do business with when I represented the Milwaukee Road, and as they agreed, I became a consultant to others as well. It was for a period of approximately three to four months.

After that, I returned to being retired full time. After a short time, I received another phone call from my friend asking if I could meet him over at Sentry World Golf Course to play a round of golf with him. I suspected he wanted to talk with me about something important.

I hung up the phone and I told Neva I was going to receive a job offer while we were playing golf, so Neva and I figured out an amount that I would not go to work for, and if it was higher than that amount, I might accept it depending on the offer. When he made the offer the salary was such that it wasn't difficult to say yes.

On my way back home, I called Neva and told her what time I should arrive home and that we would go out for dinner. She asked what happened, and I told her I was offered a job and had accepted.

She asked, "How much?"

I replied, "Remember the amount we talked about? Well, I'll give you that and I'll keep the rest."

Neva replied, "We'll talk about that later, but I'm glad to hear it was that good of a meeting."

***

For a while I worked out of my house, but then moved down to their Chicago office. The agreement was for two years, and before the end of that term, I was to train a replacement. They also arranged for the sale of our house, so we didn't have to worry about it. I was to be Director, Intermodal Sales and responsible for all TOFC and COFC traffic throughout the US and Canada.

In 1988, the National Association of Shipper Agents held their annual convention in Maui, Hawaii, and I took Neva with me to attend it. The first night we were there, before the convention started, I met a customer from Canada we had done business with when I worked for the Milwaukee Road. When he heard I was out of retirement and working for a new railroad, he said he would switch business he had going to Vancouver via the Chicago & Northwestern Railroad to our railroad, if I could meet the rate he was using.

I called the manager working for me and told him to call our connection in Canada to see if they would agree to work with us on this movement, and they did. The next day when I saw the customer I told him we agreed to the rate and gave him a copy of the agreement. The business was ours, and was worth the expense of the convention.

After the convention was over, Neva and I took a week of vacation on the Island of Oahu. I enjoyed the time with her and we had a lot of fun.

In September of 1989, I was severed from the company, according to the agreement. The next day I called the Railroad Retirement Board in Chicago and told them I was no longer working for the railroad, and was applying for reinstatement of my railroad retirement pension. Was that ever a mess?

I was having a horrible time trying to get my railroad retirement pension reinstated, even calling my congressman and senators that couldn't help me, and all three of them useless as far as help was concerned.

In calling the Chicago office of the Railroad Retirement Board, a woman answered and I explained again what I needed.

She told me that I didn't have any idea of how much work I was making them do, as they had to go back to when I first started working for the railroad in 1943, and go through all the records every year until the present, to work out what I should now receive.

Finally in December of that same year, we

received our first retirement check. It covered October, November and December. The monthly checks were about $50.00 to $75.00 more than what I had received previously, before I went back to work for the new railroad.

Neva and I thought it should be a lot more than that, but when I called them to recheck the numbers, they replied that it was correct. We never argued with them anymore.

Eighteen years and seven months from the day our pensions should have been done correctly and sent to us, Neva and I each received a letter from the Railroad Retirement Board in Chicago that an error occurred in figuring our new pensions, and they were sending us checks to bring it up to date and had sent the correct tax money from our pension payment to the IRS.

As we had our pension checks sent direct to our checking account, I called our bank and asked them to see if any large deposits were made to our account. The personal banker checked, came back on the phone and said, "Would a deposit of over $45, 000.00 be unusual?"

I replied, "I believe so." The federal taxes they withheld was over $13,000.00, so it wasn't difficult to see what the size of their error amounted to. From then on, our pensions increased by $200.00 per month, which isn't bad. I put in a request for it, but they wouldn't pay any interest on the money they never properly paid us.

***

When I was severed by the carrier I worked for, we had to stay in Chicago from October 1989 to March 1990, as we had to honor our lease on the house we rented. Then we moved back to the Green Bay area as we found a very nice apartment in Ashwaubenon, a suburb of Green Bay.

An old friend of mine started the Green Bay Experienced Traffic Club while I was gone, so when I retired in the city, he asked me to join. I was happy to do so. The next year I was Secretary of the GBETC, and in time I became president of it.

The same thing happened when he asked me to join the Ancient Order of Pine Snakes. I ended up being the president for a year. That was a philanthropy club, where we all sat around a table and made decisions on who should receive our money. One day, a friend of one of the members walked in and said, "So this is the place where you're playing poker at," spoiling the rest of the day. Now we have to be careful how we explain what we do when the club meets.

***

Back in June of 1985, I was playing golf when I

started to notice I was having difficulty walking the last few holes. It first started on the 9th hole but eventually it worked its way backwards to the 8th, 7th and 6th holes. My legs were not only in pain, but the back side of my legs were getting hard. If I was going to play any more golf, I would have to use a riding cart.

Then the real shocker came. I couldn't "perform" anymore when I was with Neva. I went to see our primary doctor we had at the time, but he had no idea what was wrong with me. I also saw an urologist, who didn't know, either. We never connected the two problems together, and not knowing where to go for help, we lived with it.

We didn't get the real truth of what happened until almost twenty-five years later from a radiologist in Green Bay.

We had lived in Ashwaubenon for approximately nine years and then moved to the Village of Howard, another suburb of Green Bay, where we also had a very nice apartment and lived there for approximately nine years. It was during this time I was running into more trouble with my legs.

I was going to the veterans clinic in Appleton, Wisconsin, about thirty minutes away from home and I had a very good doctor. He tried to figure out what was wrong, but couldn't, so he sent me to doctors who specialized in various problems of the body.

They couldn't find anything wrong with me, either. One doctor that checked my spine found a bulging disc, but advised that it wouldn't effect what I was going through or give the symptoms I was having.

Then, my doctor at the VA clinic said he wanted me to see a Doctor Richard McNutt, who was a vascular specialist and surgeon in Green Bay, who would know what was wrong with me, if anyone would.

I agreed to see Doctor McNutt, and it didn't take him very long to know what was wrong. I had Peripheral Artery Disease, also known as PAD. He ordered an angiogram to be given me to see where any blockages were in my body. He told me I had two choices, be operated on or go on a walking regimen, where I was to walk until I couldn't go any further, and then walk a little further. I choose the latter.

When I started walking, I couldn't go any further than 200 steps. As I continued on the plan, I built it up until I could walk 1350 steps, and that was when I hit the wall. From there, I started going back down in the number of steps I could do. He advised it was time to operate.

When I asked Doctor McNutt about the pros and cons, he didn't sugar coat it as some people would. He gave it to me straight, and I appreciated him for it. Either surgery, or my life would be considerably shorter.

The surgery was done on a Monday. Doctor McNutt cut open the main artery in my left leg, scraped out the blockage, which he told me was so bad the blood was going through a drop at a time, and then put the artery back together again.

I was in the hospital until the following Saturday, which surprised me as I had friends who had heart by-pass surgery that were out in three days. I have all the faith in the world in Doctor McNutt, and I also consider him a friend that I can talk with to this day.

Periodically, I've been back in the hospital having stents put in different arteries due to blockages. This one time after they put in a stent, the radiologist came to my room to talk with me, and I finally learned what had caused my problem back in July of 1985. He advised that while watching the flow of the dye in my arteries he noticed it was stopped at an artery that's near the groin that feeds the genitals. He advised that artery was blocked solid and there was no way he could do any angioplasty or place a stent in there.

Later, I asked Doctor McNutt if he could operate on that specific artery like he had in my leg, and he advised he was sorry but there was no way it could be done, due to the location of the artery.

It's now been approximately thirty-one years and we didn't let it affect us or our marriage, thanks to my wonderful wife. So far I have five stents in the lower half of my body, and there is another artery that will need to be scraped out if I live long enough and it gets bad enough. I hope Doctor McNutt is still available to do the job as I know I'll get the best care possible, which he has done for me a number of times in the past.

***

Earlier in the book I referred to looking for golf balls as we didn't have the money to buy them. During my retirement and playing the amount of golf, I had wonderful times when I could really hunt for balls, and believe me, we found them. I was keeping my sister, Ardyth's husband, Bob, supplied with all the titlists he needed.

One day I received a call from him asking if I had any extra balls available. I said, "Yes, quite a few, you need more?"

He replied, "No, but we went to our bank and they are collecting golf clubs and golf balls to send over to Iraq so the soldiers could hit them on a driving range."

I said, "Hell, I can send them a lot of golf balls, and I know where to get more. I'll put out an e-mail to all of the people on my railroad address book and I'm sure they'll come through for something like that."

Then a short time ago, our daughter, Marcia, sent me an e-mail she had found about the golf ball/golf club event the bank held. It was a letter that Sgt. 1st Class Wendy Butts, Multi-National Corps-Iraq, Photojournalist sent on January 29, 2008 telling about it. She wrote about how Gail Meintzer, a retired railroad worker, from Green Bay had learned about the Support Our Troops project from family members in Hinsdale, Illinois.

I hadn't realized it at the time, but hundreds of people would learn about this project due to the email that I sent out to my friends in the railroad. Together, the troops received hundreds of golf balls and golfing equipment. It was a proud moment for me seeing the article and what my friends of the railroad had been able to accomplish together for the United States military.

***

In 1997, our children had a dinner party for us on our 50th wedding anniversary. In the afternoon, we renewed our vows in the park in Bartlett, Illinois, and the dinner was held in St. Charles, Illinois. It was a nice June day, and it was wonderful having all our children and their families present for the event.

A few years later, we received an invitation to attend our grandson Mitchell's wedding on April

4, 2009. It was one of the last long trips Neva and I made. We left home in plenty of time so we could visit for a few days prior to the wedding. It was a very nice church wedding and the bride, Rebecca, looked beautiful. The reception was held at their home in Irving, Texas on a wonderful sunny day, and we had a great time.

One of our daughters, Marcia, asked me to dance with her, and awhile later, Rebecca asked me to dance with her. I understand Rebecca didn't have any grandfathers, as they passed away prior to her birth, and she told me she looked forward to having me as her grandpa. (I kidded with Rebecca, as she asked all of the male relatives to grow a beard for her wedding. Then, I had to renew my Wisconsin driver's license which is good from January, 2009 through March, 2017. It still shows me with a beard in the picture, although I haven't had a beard to my chin in years.)

Neva and I were sitting at a table with some family members and many of Rebecca's and Mitch's friends, who we have known for several years when there was a lull in our conversation. I heard our grandson speaking, and while I didn't hear every word he said, I did catch him saying something. "I try to model myself after Grandpa Gail, as I have never met a more honest person or a person who has more integrity than him." It touched my heart.

When the company Mitchell was working for

wanted to transfer him across the country to a new position several times, he would call me for advice, as I had a lot of experience in moving with all the transfers I had working for the railroad. That evening, when we had a little time alone together, he and I had a nice conversation. I told him how I appreciated the comments he said about me, and he told me, "I've looked up to the way you've progressed through your career and looked to you for counsel in my career, and hoped to be half the man that you are."

My hopes are that he, and my other grandsons becomes better men than I am. It certainly looks like Mitchell will be accomplished from his actions when he was running in the Boston Marathon in April, 2016.

As he was approaching the finish line, a runner ahead of him started showing signs of distress flopping his arms, swaying, and finally collapsed. As Mitchell reached him, he told the runner, "You raced this far, I'll see that you cross the finish line."

As he was helping the man, another runner came over and assisted Mitchell in getting him across the finish line and then the medics took the runner to the hospital. The man's temperature was 108 degrees, and the word came out that the man would have died if Mitchell and the other runner hadn't helped him.

It made national news on TV and headlines in

the Boston papers. We're very proud of him, as well as the other grandchildren we have. We have two grandsons, Marshall, now a police officer, and Matthew, now a college professor, who both served in the US Army; two grandsons, Zach, now working for a company in the atomic industry, was on a US Navy atomic submarine, and Chris, who runs his own company was in the US Navy Seabees. Our granddaughter, Amanda, was a graduate of the Air Force Academy and then a major in the US Air Force flying helicopters in the Iraq war before she resigned her commission to reenter civilian life. She works in a library in Albuquerque, New Mexico.

Our granddaughter, Samantha, is a registered nurse, along with being a wife and mother. Melissa, another granddaughter, is a wife and mother of three sons; Jacob and Luke were born with Cystic Fibroses and manages their health. And Luke is at the Pittsburgh Clinic having just received a double lung transplant. Our grandsons, Andrew, who is taking three majors at the University of Illinois; and Dustin, studying to become a mortician, both in college as well as working, and our youngest granddaughter, Tyler, who is a senior in high school and working part-time. As I mentioned earlier, a group of people Neva and I are very proud of.

***

Someone asked me what my favorite place to play golf was once, and I really had to think about it for a while. I've played on courses all over the country as well as in Canada and Hawaii. The course we lived on—Briargate Country Club was number one in my mind, but that is not playable any more for me, as it is now a private club.

Keeping in mind that I'm an old man now, I would have to say Mid Vallee Golf Course, as the owners made it playable for all golfers, putting in senior tees on the long holes. Now that I don't play golf with friends for money anymore, and just play for the fun of it, my age allows me to change the rules to what I like. And if you're out there, you will probably see me playing from any tee I feel like at the time.

My thought is I'll play from any tee, so I can reach the fairway with my drive. Then I'm back to playing by the rules. If you're one of the golfers that thinks you have to play from the back tees when you're not qualified to do so, all you do is back up play and make it slow for all of the golfers behind you.

We were having lunch with our son, Doug, when I told him I was thinking of playing golf one time in September, and that would be my final round of golf. He said he wanted to play that round with me, which I was happy to hear. I've handed over my golf equipment to him, just as I did my bowling equipment.

Anyone that has exchanged e-mails with me always sees "Keep it in the Fairway" on all of my e-mails. It's my favorite quote. I played with a lot of fellows that could out-hit me for distance, but I usually kept it in the fairway and was always competitive with the long hitters because of it.

Recently, I was also asked about my philosophies.

A person has two things he or she has complete control of, and that is their honesty and integrity, and you never want to lose it. I learned a long time ago to not deliberately lie. If you make a mistake, its best to admit it, with comments similar to: I erred, I blew it, I didn't see that and it's my fault, etc. If you get caught lying, you lose the respect of those involved, and that can spread to others.

Another thing is, don't brag when you win. I learned that when I played pool with a cousin of mine when I was in high school. After beating him really badly after a few games and rubbing it in, he made a single comment that woke me up. He looked at me and commented, "I'm not a pool hall bum like you are, and walked away." That hurt, and I deserved it. I learned a lesson the hard way and never forgot it.

I worked for forty-two years in the railroad industry minus three years in the military, and loved working for the railroad. I looked forward to going to work each day, as there would be new problems to face and overcome, new people to meet, and new things to work on. I don't know how it could be any better than that.

I hear people comment about hating to go to work, or if I didn't have to do this or that, what a drag this is, and then I think to myself how lucky I was to start working for a company that had so much to offer. I was so fortunate to see that, and with hard work, put myself in positions so my superiors noticed me and moved me upward and forward.

I've been told there are two things you should never talk about in business—religion and politics. As far as I can recall, I can't remember doing so in business. I know that since I retired, I have stepped on toes when it comes to politics. One reason is the fact I have a wife and four daughters, four granddaughters, and three great granddaughters, and I want those women to be treated as equals to any man or let them attempt to be equals to any man, as well as have control over their health and bodies.

I don't believe you should vote for someone because your parents, relative or friend votes a certain way. It's my belief you should vote for what you believe in, what will affect you and your family, and if you are married, it's senseless to split your vote. You might as well not vote as to split it, as you are off-setting each other. Yet I know some couples do it, as they don't take the time to talk about it in advance.

From what I've read, people that are gay are born that way, due to something that happened when they were conceived or in the mother's womb. I had a gay gentleman working for me when I headed up the Des Moines, Iowa office. He was a good worker and a real gentleman, and everyone in the transportation industry knew him and liked him. While I knew him, he had a partner for thirty-five years, and the only thing that stopped their continuing together longer was the death of one of them.

I often hear people talking about gays in a harsh manner, which bothers me. Whether or not I know the person, I will usually look directly at them and comment, "Since you don't appear to think well of gays, what are you going to do if one of your young children or grandchildren comes up to you and says, "Dad or Grandpa, I want you to be the first to know that I'm gay. What are you going to do, throw him or her under the bus?" I love to see the look on their face after I say that to them. Sometimes, there's just too much ignorance.

***

In 2012, a dinner party was held for our 65th wedding anniversary in De Pere, Wisconsin, another suburb of Green Bay, where Neva and I now live. Most of our extended family were present along with my sister, Ardyth, and her children. We had an enjoyable time talking with those we don't see frequently.

I have had several different doctors at the veterans clinic, and I had confidence in each of them, which to me is very important. I also decided I should have a local doctor in case of emergencies, and as my wife, Neva, was going to Doctor Mark Jenson, I asked if I could also become his patient. He advised he would be happy to have me as a patient.

For a while it was the normal yearly check-up, but when I started having stomach problems, he told me to have an endoscopic examination. When they did it, they found I had a bleeding ulcer and had lost a lot of blood due to taking a low dose of aspirin over a very long time. We got that corrected, and I'm now using medicine to protect my stomach from having it happen again.

On a visit to Doctor Jenson one day, I mentioned I was having difficulty sleeping at night as my right shoulder was hurting when I laid on my right side, and when I laid on my left side my hip hurt. He commented, "Let's take some x-rays," and they showed I needed a hip replacement and had a broken collar bone. I saw the x-ray myself and still can't believe I broke my shoulder blade.

The doctor suggested doing the hip replacement first and the shoulder second, as it feels like you have been hit by a truck when you have a shoulder operated on. In my invincible wisdom I said, shoulder first. I have to be able to move around, as I have so many things to do. WRONG AGAIN. I heard someone say swing your arm front and back, and you will be able to move your arm straight up and that's it. It was, but I couldn't wash my left shoulder as I couldn't get my hand and arm across my chest to my left side. Back to the doctor and I ended up with 17 weeks of therapy. Another great decision. Next time, I'll think things through.

***

A couple of years ago, we were having a very hot summer and I was sweating a lot, but Neva was continually cold so we didn't use the air conditioning every much. Neva had an appointment with Doctor Jenson in the last days of September, and it was getting a little cooler but I was still sweating profusely. When she was done, I asked the doctor if he had any idea of why I was sweating so much. He told me he was going to have me take an EKG check. After it was finished, he told me to go back to where Neva was and he would see me in a few minutes.

A few minutes later, he came in and asked me, "Do you know Doctor Todd Fergus across the street from here?"

I said, "Yes, as I received a Stress Test a number of years ago," along with a number of other procedures.

Doctor Jenson said, "Good, you have an appointment tomorrow morning at 10 a.m. with him and don't miss it, as you are in trouble."

I went to see Doctor Fergus and he told me he is at St. Vincent's Hospital on Mondays and St. Mary's on Wednesday. Which day would be best?

I said, "Monday at St. Vincent's," and the next Monday he did the procedure on me.

After he was finished doing procedures for the day, Doctor Fergus came to my room where I was recovering and told me I had three blockages in the arteries leading from my heart. The east main artery was blocked 80 %, and an artery in the back of my heart had two blockages, one was 96% and the other was 99%. He advised they call it "The Widow Maker" and that's what it does, it makes your wife a widow.

I didn't even know I was sick, as I had no warning signs like pain in my chest or arms, or shortness of breath. I commented that now I know why I never win the lottery, as I was using all my "luck" to stay alive.

Then when I had an appointment with my dermatologist, Doctor Michelle Cihla, she saw indications that I had skin cancer, so she cut a V shape piece of flesh out of my left arm and the diagnoses showed two different types of cancer in what she cut out. Doctor Cihla must also be an excellent seamstress as she did a beautiful job sewing the cut area together so you can't even see where she cut me. My thanks goes to the good doctor.

When Neva and I were young, we didn't know about cancer like they do now, and we didn't realize the problems that would come up later in our life. That was the second procedure of skin cancer I had.

The day before Thanksgiving last year (2015), I was feeling very light-headed, so we called 9-1-1 and when they checked me at home, my blood pressure indicated I needed hospital care. I spent that day and half of Thanksgiving in St. Vincent's hospital, as they found I had atrial fibrillation. For the next thirty days, I had to wear a heart monitor that transmitted how my heart was doing during this time span.

The doctors ascertained that I now have to take Warfarin to keep my blood thin enough so I don't have a stroke or heart attack, and thick enough so I don't bleed to death. Neva has to have the same medicine, so we have appointments with Doctor Jenson every month. If the blood tests are bad, we have two appointments that month.

With so many things wrong, and having to forgo different foods and other food stuffs, it's difficult to find things I can eat when we go out to eat, as well as buying food to eat at home. For years I ate the same cereal for breakfast, and now I have to be very careful about the amount of sodium I consume. I looked at the package of my favorite cereal and saw it contained 160 MGs of sodium. Now I eat a frosted wheat cereal with 0 MGs of sodium. It's healthier.

***

On Saturday, June 18th, 2016 we sat down with four of our five children and celebrated our 69th wedding anniversary that fell on Tuesday, June 21st. Our daughter, Linda, was missing, as she and our grandson Lucas were still in Pittsburgh at the Pittsburgh clinic, as Lucas received a double lung transplant and must stay there as he recovers from his operation. He can go back to their temporary apartment in Pittsburgh, with the plan to return to Illinois in two months' time.

Our children gave us a large number of grandchildren: Matthew, Melissa, Mitchell, Amanda, Marshall, Zachery, Christopher, Samantha, twins Jacob and Lucas, Andrew, Dustin and Tyler. And these grandchildren gave us great grandchildren: Malachai, Simon, Victoria, Olivia, Miles, Owen, William, Nora and Charlie, and I would be surprised if there wouldn't be more in the future.

Our grandchildren also married into the family the following grandchildren-in-laws: Matthew -Ailene, Melissa - Brad, Mitchell - Rebecca, Marshall - Ashley, Christopher - Katie, and Samantha brought in Chris, and we are proud to have them join our extended family.

We do have a step-grandchild, Douglas' Melissa. And also some step-great grandchildren. Matthew has Jacque and Mason, Marshall has Greyson, and Douglas has Rhian and Keiran.

I would feel remiss if I didn't mention my sister, Ardyth's children, as they have been a large part of our family. Warren and his wife Cheryl, Bill and his wife Debbie, and Chris and her husband, Mike. We enjoy my niece and nephews very much. I am also sorry about the untimely passing of my nephew Robert and niece, Carole. We considered both as part of our extended family and enjoyed the times we spent together.

We have one more *detour* to make, and that will be from DePere, Wisconsin to Dundee, Illinois.

Neva and I have given orders to our children through our Trust what we want done when we expire. We'll be cremated, with no wake, funeral, or memorial service. The cremains of the first of us to die will be held until the other expires, is cremated, and then both of our cremains will be mixed together in one vault and buried in a cemetery in Dundee, Illinois, so we will still be together for ever in eternity. We have also arranged for the remaining of extended family to have a "Celebration of Life" for us so they can have a "hell of a party" on us, as I've always enjoyed a good party.

I've experienced a lot of things during my life, enjoyed most of them, and figured out how to live with the rest. From now until then, we will live our lives together and enjoy what we can and hope for the best, and be sure to "Keep it in the Fairway."

Neva and Gail Meintzer, 2007
Retired in Green Bay, WI

Meintzer Family, 1997

Meintzer Family, 2014

Gail and Neva Meintzer and family, July 2014

Ardyth Haws, Gail and Neva Meintzer, July 2014

Acknowledgements

For all the veterans and railroaders I had the pleasure to work with and know, thank you for your friendship and assistance over the years.

For my family, to my children, grandchildren, and great grandchildren, this book happened because of all of your questions.

Thank you to my sister, Ardyth, for always being there, supporting me, and being the best sister anyone could ask for.

And thanks to Kaye Ambrose, for the introduction to your daughter, Brittiany Koren, my editor, who took interest in my story, assisted me personally, and published my book.

About the Author

Gail F. Meintzer started working for the railroad system before he was drafted into the US Army for World War II, and he served again during the Korean War. Married to Neva Jewell in 1947, they had five children together. He retired as Director, Intermodal Sales from Milwaukee Road in 1985, helped start the Wisconsin Central Ltd. (Railroad) in 1987, and after teaching a man to take his position in the railroad, retired in September, 1989. Today, Gail and Neva have 13 grandchildren and 9 great grandchildren. They celebrated their 69th wedding anniversary on June 21st, 2016 in Green Bay, Wisconsin. To contact Mr. Meintzer, please visit www.writtendreams.com.